REMOTE CONTROL RETIREMENT RICHES

HOW TO CHANGE YOUR FUTURE WITH RENTAL HOMES

What People Are Saying About Adiel Gorel

"I retired ten years ago, thanks in part to the large number of investment homes I had bought with Adiel's help. Local property managers take care of my out-of-state rental home investments. Those remote property managers make it effortless." —*John S., retired CPA*

"My story is one of buying and thinking long-term: I've been able to pay off the mortgages on almost all of my properties. I now own over a dozen paid-off rentals in great markets. I obviously have a very positive cash flow. This collection of single-family homes has become my main nest egg. Adiel's guidance and assistance has had a profound effect on me. It enabled me to enjoy a semi-retirement." —*Bradley H., MD*

"At age 80, I have been retired for over a decade, in a fashion I never dreamt would have been possible, largely on the strength of my single-family home rentals bought with Adiel's advice. My advice: Don't doubt yourself. I'm living proof that it can be done." —*Peter S., retired educator*

REMOTE CONTROL RETIREMENT RICHES

HOW TO CHANGE YOUR FUTURE WITH RENTAL HOMES

Adiel Gorel

PROGRESS PRESS
SAN RAFAEL, CALIFORNIA

Progress Press
165 North Redwood Drive, Ste #150
San Rafael, CA 94903
icgre.com
info@icgre.com

Publisher's Note: This publication contains the ideas and opinions of its author. The strategies outlined in this book may not be suitable for every individual and are not guaranteed or warranted to produce any particular results. No warranty is made with respect to the accuracy or completeness of the information contained herein, and both the author and the publisher specifically disclaim any responsibility for any liability, loss or risk, personal or otherwise, which is incurred as a consequence, directly or indirectly, of the use and application of any of the contents of this book.

Ordering Information:
Quantity sales. Special discounts are available on quantity purchases by corporations, associations, and others. For details, contact the "Special Sales Department" at the address above.

Remote Control Retirement Riches: How to Change Your Future with Rental Homes / Adiel Gorel. This is the 2021 revised edition of *Remote Controlled Real Estate Riches: The Busy Person's Guide to Real Estate Investing*, originally published in 2001.

Names: Gorel, Adiel, author.
Title: Remote control retirement riches : how to change your future with rental homes / Adiel Gorel.
Description: Includes index. | San Rafael, CA: Progress Press, 2021.
Identifiers: LCCN: 2021906371| ISBN: 978-1-7324494-6-6
Subjects: LCSH Real estate investment--United States. | Retirement--Planning. | Retirement income--United States. | Real property. | Finance, Personal. | BISAC BUSINESS & ECONOMICS / Real Estate. Classification: LCC HD1379 .G67 2021 | DDC 332.6/324--dc23

For the memory of
Ed and Connie Bergeson
My first property managers
And dear friends

ACKNOWLEDGMENTS

Since I wrote my first book in 2001, I have gotten countless requests to update it, revise it, and bring it to current times.

And it took a village to accomplish that task!

Many thanks to the ICG staff, in the U.S. and abroad, for their constant support of our investors, and for making the operation run smoothly, enabling me to have the time to create this book as well as a second book (*Invest Then Rest*) in the same timeframe.

Thanks to our market teams, all over the U.S., who have been tirelessly finding great single-family rental homes for us in the best locations. The support you have given our investors, as well as myself and our staff, is very much appreciated, along with your providing up-to-date examples for this revised book.

I would like to extend special thanks to the local property management teams in our various markets, who make it truly possible to own good rental homes in the best markets, even if the owner lives in another state, or even another country. Your professional practices are exemplary and are featured in this book.

I would like to thank our investors, from whom I keep learning over the years. I appreciate you for your determination, "do-it" attitude, and getting me inspired by how you have changed your lives following this simple method. Your experiences, reports, and sharing, has helped me improve our system and make it simpler and better for everyone, and helped me improve this book immeasurably.

Thanks to Meir Stein and Tsah Itic for going over the book and sharing your feedback with me. It helped me make it better.

Thanks to Paul Pavlovich for the delightful artwork for this book and the other materials created to support our investors and raise money for public television.

Thanks to Ruth Schwartz, who as my book midwife, editor and design project manager patiently got me through the rounds of revisions on this book as well as a second book and all of the public television package materials, helping me keep track and meet our deadlines.

Thanks to Erin Saxton, Chad LeFevre, Jerry Adams, and Debbie and Chad Cox for widening the platform, making our message reach more people, helping them change their futures.

And last but not least, special thanks to my children, Daphne and Daniel. You are a constant source of inspiration, I keep learning from you, and I appreciate that you also tolerate your often-busy Dad. I love you!

Design: Paul Pavlovich
Photos courtesy of Shutterstock.com

CONTENTS

PREFACE

If you're like most Americans, you're too busy earning a living to set up a secure retirement. When you add the demands of home and family, it's amazing that you've got time left over to do anything at all, much less think about your financial future.

Perhaps this scenario sounds familiar: you and your spouse are in your early fifties and have two children, one is finishing middle school, and one in high school. You've read about escalating college expenses and you're worried. Your parents are retired and may need your financial support in the coming years. You'd like to retire yourself in 15 years or so, and it's suddenly occurred to you (in those few spare minutes between work, school plays, soccer games, and taking the dog to the vet) that it's going to take a lot more than your income to meet all these demands.

For some people, panic sets in. They imagine that the only way they're going to get ahead is to make a small fortune—preferably overnight.

Real estate books and videos that promise quick riches take advantage of the alarm you may feel when you contemplate your future. In real estate particularly, you may be told that you can find a "perfect deal" that's going to make you wealthy. All you have to do is locate a bargain property that's worth twice what you offer and sell it for a huge profit. Twenty years can go by before a deal like that comes around, if it ever does. You can waste years trying to become an overnight millionaire—years you could have spent actually becoming a millionaire.

Between work, family and (hopefully) an occasional vacation, how are you going to find that bargain property and the "perfect" deal? It's not surprising that many potential real estate investors simply give up. Real estate get-rich-quick schemes may seem enticing at first, but it soon becomes clear that in order to reap the promised rewards, you have to become as expert as the experts, which means devoting your life to your investments.

But who has the time for that? More to the point, who wants to?

It is possible to build wealth through real estate, especially via the powerful yet very simple vehicle of single-family rental homes in affordable markets, and it isn't contingent upon overnight success, finding the "perfect" deal or becoming an expert. *Remote Control Retirement Riches* is a book for those who have no interest in giving up their current career, or even all their nights and weekends, to play the real estate game. For those who prefer to put their family, work and life first, while keeping their investments on track with a minimum expenditure of time. *Remote Control Retirement Riches* will show you that you don't have to spend your weekends hunting down bargain properties, managing tenants, collecting rent, or repairing the proverbial leaky toilet in order to make safe, sound real estate investments that will secure your financial future.

Since 1987, I've worked with thousands of people just like you and purchased several thousand homes for investors and myself. I've learned the rules of successful, "hands-off" real estate investing, and distilled them down to a simple, streamlined method that's proven itself again and again. Having helped thousands over more than three decades, the results are in. Many lives have changed for the better, people sent kids or grandkids to college, retired securely, and some chose to build vast wealth by doing more of the same.

Anyone can benefit from my experience and the experience of other investors and use this method to build a single-family home portfolio that will have a profound impact on his or her family's financial well-being.

I'll tell you what to buy, where to buy, and how to buy rental homes in a fashion that's manageable within the framework of your busy lifestyle.

I'll show you how to get started, how to make a plan based on your current commitments and future needs, and how to work with real estate professionals so that your most valuable resource—your time—is not wasted.

I'm not going to tell you that you can make millions of dollars overnight, with your first deal, or even within the first year (although I know a number of investors who have). But with *Remote Control Retirement Riches*, you'll discover that creating financial abundance while not giving up your day-to-day life is something that you can accomplish, regardless of your present circumstances.

CHAPTER 1

EVERYONE NEEDS AN INVESTMENT PLAN (YES, EVEN YOU)

In the film *The Graduate,* an older man taps the young hero on the shoulder and offers some sage advice: "I've got one thing to say to you: plastics."

In 1968, this wasn't bad counsel. Since the film ends after Benjamin Braddock rescues Elaine Robinson from a loveless marriage, we'll never know if he secured his future with a career in plastics or founded an ecologically friendly and extremely profitable recycling firm. But we all know that Ben wasn't thinking about the future much. In fact, he spent most of his time trying to avoid thinking about it.

Fortunately for Ben, he was a character in a movie.

You and I don't have the same good fortune. After we win the heart of the woman or man of our dreams, life goes on (and usually gets a lot more complicated). I'm going to give you a figurative tap on the shoulder and offer some sage advice:

I've got one thing to say to you: financial planning.

Financial planning? What, you may wonder, does that have to do with real estate investing?

Everything. *Remote Control Retirement Riches* isn't about a mythical pot of gold at the end of the rainbow. It's about creating the life you want while not requiring you to give up your day-to-day life. It's about building wealth so that your future is everything you want it to be.

The Empty Channel

Each of us lives in two channels: one where we work, live, earn, and spend, and another where we build for the future with savings and investments. For many, the second channel is nearly empty. It's not surprising, because most of us weren't taught much about investing. Words like "financial goals" and "retirement plan" seem to belong to Wall Street experts, not us. In today's world, however, these are words you need to become familiar with—the sooner you begin, the better off you'll be.

In 1981, I came to the U.S. to finish my graduate studies in electrical engineering at Stanford University. I was a poor student, here on a scholarship. When I finished graduate school, I got a job nearby at Hewlett-Packard Laboratories.

Two things happened when I got my first job. First, I felt rich all of a sudden—there was a big difference between my scholarship stipend and a Silicon Valley engineer's salary. Second, many of my colleagues had been there for 15 or 25 years. Yet, almost without exception, they didn't have much to show for those long years of work. Although they were well paid, they didn't have much in terms of their financial net worth. Typically, they owned a home, two cars, and had a 401(k).

I saw immediately that with their salary and credit scores, they could have been financially independent after 15 or 25 years. Why weren't they? Because no one had shown them it was possible. Who knows how different their situation could have been if only they'd thought about the future and created a financial plan of their own.

Especially for those of you who hate to balance your checkbook, the words "financial" and "planning" in tandem can be as welcome as a visit to the dentist. There are certain things in life almost no one likes to do. Taxes, for instance. Of course, if you don't pay your taxes, you could wind up in prison. As things stand, no one's going to throw you in jail for lack of a little financial planning, so it's a lot easier to overlook.

But I'm here to tell you financial planning is as important as sending in your tax return each year. Without it, you might end up in a place you don't want to be: 65 (or 75+), retired, and living on a small, fixed income.

Regardless of your specific goals, one aspect of financial planning is the same for all of us, and that's retirement planning. Even if retirement seems, at present, a long way off there will come a time when you no longer wish to—or can't—work any longer.

Retirement in the New Millennium

Do you remember when your grandfather retired? Chances are, when he turned 65, the company where he'd worked for 40 years threw him a party and gave him a gold watch. He received a pension that, along with Social Security benefits, allowed him to live comfortably in his "golden years."

I think I'm safe in assuming that this kind of retirement isn't in your future. We all know life has changed enormously in the past 50 years. In 1970, the things we now take for granted—personal computers, smart phones, streaming services, microwave ovens, even the Internet— belonged in a Jetson's cartoon, not in our homes. While the technological innovations of the 21st century are the most obvious indicators of change, our lifestyle has shifted dramatically, too. And one of the most dramatic areas is in how—and how well—we'll retire.

If you're just beginning to realize your retirement years might be less "golden" than you'd like, you have a lot of company. Anyone born between 1946 and 1964—belonging to the Baby Boomer generation, and beyond, Gen X, Millennials, and Gen Z—is facing a vastly different future from that of their parents and grandparents. We can't rely on employers or the government to provide for us once we stop working. If we don't do it ourselves, it won't happen.

What Pension?

The truth is most of us don't stick around for the gold watch. Careers are more often made by changing companies than climbing a single corporate ladder. Mergers and downsizing also add to frequent job changes.

401(k) retirement plans have taken the place of many company pension plans. While a 401(k) has the benefit of moving with you when you change jobs, it also means half the contributions come from your paycheck. The increasing numbers of freelancers, entrepreneurs, and consultants don't even have the advantage of an employer's 50% contribution they must rely solely on their own contributions to a government-sponsored retirement plan.

If you start contributing to a 401(k) or Keogh (for self-employed individuals) in your twenties or early thirties, you can conceivably amass enough wealth to be comfortable when you retire—but regardless of how much you put aside, inflation can wreak havoc on your nest egg. Unfortunately, I've found most people don't even begin thinking about retirement until they're at least in their forties...and perhaps not even then.

Social Security

Here too, there's a very good chance that what worked for our parents and grandparents isn't going to work for us. Currently, Social Security provides a maximum of $3,011 per month if one retires at the full retirement age—and that's only if you contributed the maximum amount during your lifetime.

My family, in the San Francisco Bay Area, couldn't live on $3,011 per month—could yours? And due to the changing demographics of our society, these benefits aren't likely to increase much. About seven years ago, Baby Boomers began retiring en masse; a retirement wave expected to continue for at least another decade. As the years pass, only two workers will be paying into the program for every retiree who's taking money out. Unless there are drastic changes in the system, Social Security will not provide you with a comfortable retirement (unless you enjoy clipping coupons and buying groceries with food stamps).

Longer Life Spans

In 1970, the average life expectancy was 60 to 65. In fact, the entire Social Security system was based upon this life span. It meant that benefits would be paid out to only some individuals, and then only for a few years.

Today's average life expectancy is closer to 80. And who knows what the next 20 years will bring? Healthier lifestyles, medical advances, and biotechnology could easily push the average up to 100. Even today, there exists a genetic editor called CRISPR (Clustered Regularly Interspaced Short Palindromic Repeats), with the ability to actually change undesirable genes. In fact, the two scientists responsible for the development of CRISPR received the Nobel Prize in 2020. In the near future, it is very likely that such technology will be widely available, potentially increasing lifespans dramatically. Nanotechnology holds the future promise of repairing old cells and bringing them to full health again. This too can extend lifespans quite significantly.

This is an enormously important thing to consider. It means that if you retire at 65, you may need enough money to live on for 20, 30, or 40 years (and perhaps even beyond).

If that got you thinking, "I'm going to need a lot of money," you're right. And not only will it have to be a lot...it will have to be inflation-proof.

Inflation

Currently, the government estimates the annual rate of inflation is approximately 2.1%. If you remember the double-digit inflation of the early 1980s, it doesn't sound so bad, does it?

Think again. When prices rise 2.1% year after year, your purchasing power is cut by more than a quarter in only 10 years. That means your $40,000 annual salary will be worth close to $30,000 a decade hence. At a 3% rate of inflation, it will be cut by one third in a decade. At a 4% rate of inflation, it will be cut in half in 18 years.

It's startling, isn't it? But official statistics don't tell the whole story. Some things—education, housing, and healthcare have risen much more than the average rate of inflation. When all goods and services are factored in, one might argue that the inflation rate could be closer to 4-5%. In the examples, I will use lower inflation rates, so as to be conservative. As an example, let's look at some consumer prices over the years:

CONSUMER PRICES 1960–2020				
	1960	**1980**	**2000**	**2020**
Good Loaf of Bread	0.29	0.79	1.59	3.47
Gas (1 gal.) in CA	0.31	0.95	1.95	3.50
Postage stamp	0.04	0.15	0.33	0.55
Movie Tickets	2.00	4.00	8.00	14.00

As you can see, we're now paying at least twice as much for bread, gasoline, and movie tickets as we did 20 years ago. If prices continue to go up in this fashion, 20 years from now we'll be paying twice today's prices.

The unfortunate truth is the cost of some things will go up much faster than your annual cost-of-living raise. As I said earlier, not only will you need enough money to retire comfortably, you'll need an investment program that generates inflation-proof income: income that either keeps up with or exceeds the rate of inflation. And, keep in mind that during the 20 or 30 years you spend in retirement (or 40 or 50, if the average lifespan does become much longer), your expenses are likely to increase given the healthier active lifestyles people have now.

The Biggest Risk

We all know someone who's lost money on a poorly performing stock, a shaky real estate deal, or in the casinos of Las Vegas. As chancy as all these things are, there's only one that's more hazardous to your financial health: not investing wisely.

We've already seen how inflation (along with taxes, but we'll get to that later), is your money's biggest enemy. No matter how much you earn, the rising cost of living will erode your purchasing power year after year. And the bottom line truth is most of us don't have unlimited earning potential. Whether you're an auto mechanic, physician, or executive vice president, you probably have an idea of how much you can expect to bring home every year...and can count on it being pretty much the same until the day you retire. Without the bonanza of a winning lottery ticket or inheriting your rich Aunt Minnie's entire estate, how are you ever going to have enough money set aside for the inevitable time when you can't or don't want to work anymore?

A Penny Saved is Not a Penny Earned

A couple generations ago financial planning was much easier. Putting aside 10% of your income in a savings account every month was considered basic common sense, and enough to cover whatever "rainy day" might arrive. But that was before a three-day hospital stay cost nearly $100,000, and four-year college expenses hit six figures.

Even if you have the discipline to save every month (and unfortunately, studies show Baby Boomers, for example, are saving less than the two generations before them, and Millennials are not much better), it will not provide the security you'll need in your later years. In fact, allowing your money to sit in a savings account for years is the equivalent of planting an orchid in the desert: it will not grow.

Let's assume you can manage to sock away $50,000 over the next 20 years: that's saving $2500 per year. At the current (2020) interest rate for a CD account, which is under 1%, how much will you have in the bank 20 years from now? Let's even factor rising interest rates and be "generous" in assuming your CD account will get 3% in the near future. We will also be "generous" with the REAL future inflation (real measure—not what the government chooses to measure) and use 5% total inflation in this example.

The obvious answer—$50,000 plus the interest that's accrued over 20 years (in this case, $19,191)—isn't quite correct. To begin with, you must pay tax on the interest earned; if you're in the 32% tax bracket, the $19,191 you've earned in interest will be reduced by $6141, (assuming all of it is in the 32% margin), which lowers your interest earnings to $13,050.

Inflation, however, will do more damage to your savings than taxes. Inflation erodes the value of your money year after year. On the following page, the table "20 Years' Savings" shows what happens to your savings when you save at a low interest rate over a long term. In the top line, you'll see the deposited amount; the second shows the accrued 3% annual interest; the third, 32% tax on interest; the fourth, the negative effect of inflation—the amount that the value of your savings is reduced because of the rising cost of living. The final line, "Real Dollars Saved" shows what your savings will be worth in 20 years. In other words, in 20 years, your $50,000 plus interest will be worth only $30,106 in today's dollars.

20 YEARS' SAVINGS
($2500 per year, plus interest, minus tax & inflation)

	Year 1	Year 5	Year 10	Year 15	Year 20
Amount Saved	$2,500	$12,500	$25,000	$37,500	$50,000
+3% Interest (cumulative)	+$75	+$1,171	+$4,520	+$10,392	+$19,191
-32% Tax (cumulative)	-$24	-$375	-$1,446	-$3,325	-$6,141
5% Inflation (cumulative)	-$125	-$2,007	-$7,756	-$17,838	-$32,944
Real Dollars Saved	$2,426	$11,289	$20,314	$26,729	$30,106

When you discover what your money could have been doing for you during those 20 years, saving at 3% per annum is going to seem pretty foolish. Even so, some people have a hard time letting go of the savings mentality. Putting money in the bank makes them feel secure. After all, it's safe. Most people interpret this to mean risk-free, but they're wrong.

I'll say it again: the biggest risk you can take with your money is not investing it.

Imagine inflation is a train moving along a track. To keep up, you've got to move ahead at the same speed. At 5% inflation (reread the earlier sections if you are curious as to why I'm using that number), your salary must increase 5% per year. If you're just making ends meet now, your income will have to increase much more if you're going to save. Just how fast is that train going, anyway?

Chances are it's moving ahead a lot faster than you are and will be clear out of sight before you retire. It's not going to stop just because you stop working, either. The only hope you have of winning this race is to outrun the train—now and forever. And that means a long-term investment plan with an annual return greater than the rate of inflation. Or, even better, with an investment in real estate, you can allow inflation to work for you.

Worst-Case Scenarios

There are other reasons an investment plan is crucial. To paraphrase a popular bumper sticker, "Stuff happens."

None of us is exempt from life's setbacks. Divorce, the death of a spouse, costly litigation, accidents, job loss or major illness can have a devastating effect on your finances. For the most part, we don't plan for these things, because we believe they only happen to other people. Solid financial planning will not only help protect your future, it will help protect your present lifestyle.

A Vision

The whole point of this chapter was to get you thinking about your future. No one likes to contemplate getting older, but I can assure you it's much better to think about it now than later—ask anyone who's 70 or 80 and still working or trying to get by on Social Security.

Let's take you, for instance. Let's say you're 55. Think 15 years into the future. Now you're 70. Would you like to be in the same financial position you're in now?

Probably not.

Close your eyes and think on this: what if, in 15 years, you owned ten houses in your hometown free and clear? Let's say they're average homes, by today's prices: each worth $170,000. That means you'd have an estate worth $1.7 million (in today's dollar—the number in 15 years is likely to be a lot bigger). And that estate could be generating $100,000 in inflation-proof income every year.

Can you imagine how this would change your financial picture?

There's one little modification: your hometown might not be the best place to purchase your ten houses. So, instead of owning ten houses in your hometown, you'll own ten houses in the best markets in the U.S.

Impossible, you say?

But it isn't. It's much easier than you might think. Keep reading, and I'll show you how.

REPLAY

- ► Everyone needs to plan for retirement.
- ► You can't count on Social Security benefits alone.
- ► People are retiring earlier and living longer. You may need enough money to live on for 20, 30 or even 40 years and with genetics, medicine & bio-tech advances, possibly much longer.
- ► 3% inflation decreases your purchasing power by one-third in only 10 years.
- ► The biggest risk you take with your money is not investing it.
- ► Putting your money in a low-interest savings account for short-term goals is worthwhile, but when you save over the long-term, you could actually lose money.
- ► Without financial planning, life's setbacks can devastate your finances.

CHAPTER 2

WHY YOU SHOULD INVEST IN REAL ESTATE

As I said in the first chapter, this isn't just a book about real estate. It's a book about taking charge of your future, about doing something powerful with your money that can mean the difference between living your dream life and retirement poverty. It's about financial planning (those dreaded words again). And it just so happens that real estate is a great vehicle for meeting all your long-term financial needs.

Leverage (defined in the next section if you are unfamiliar with the concept), fixed-rate loans and tax deductions offer a package of benefits found in no other investment type. Historically, real estate values have increased at 1.5 times the rate of inflation (and many individual markets have exceeded that figure). That includes waves of booms and busts, for example, people in many states experienced the real estate boom of 2004-2006, as well as the recession of 2008-2011. Nevertheless, as of 2020, the majority of U.S. markets have home values higher than the very peak of 2006—sometimes by a lot. A few markets have still not fully recovered from the recession but are trending up.

Leverage

What, exactly, is leverage? It means you're using a lever, just like when you lift something heavy. In terms of money and investments, it means you're using other people's money, typically, a bank's money.

For example, if you buy a $170,000 house with a $34,000 down payment, that's 5 - 1 leverage: you're using a lever of $34,000 with a loan of $136,000 to raise $170,000. (Actual numbers would be a bit different due to loan costs and closing costs, but this gives you an idea.)

Traditionally, only real estate can be leveraged to such a degree. In the stock market, the leverage you can get is 2 - 1 (and, occasionally, 3 - 1, on selected stocks). In other words, you may be able to buy stock for only 50% of its price, with the brokerage firm providing the other 50%. This is known as buying on margin, and it is risky. If the stock dips below the price you paid for it, you may be forced to sell it—at the worst possible time—in what is known as a "margin call."

Conceivably, you can get leverage for any investment type. For example, if your mother offers to lend you 80% of the funds to buy stock, you would have 5 - 1 leverage. But when you're applying to institutions for a loan, only real estate can be leveraged 5 - 1. In 2020, under the FNMA (Federal National Mortgage Association) guidelines, the minimum down payment required for an investor buying a rental home is 15% (with PMI, or Private Mortgage Insurance). That is a leverage of 6.67 to 1.

Leverage is one of the benefits to investing in real estate: you can buy a $170,000 home for as little as 15%, or $25,500 down, or you can buy $1 million worth of real estate for only $150,000 (plus loan and closing costs in both examples). It's one of the keys to building a financially secure future. There's a saying among real estate professionals, "What you owe today, you'll own tomorrow." Why? Because after your initial 15% (or 20%) investment, the tenant pays off the remainder of the mortgage for you.

The Miracle of the American Fixed-Rate Loan

Thanks to the post-World War II strategy that enabled people to buy homes easily, we have something in this country that exists in very few places in the world: the fixed-rate loan.

The fixed-rate loan is a bonanza. It's a gift. It's incredible. When you come from another country (like me), and you see what's available in the U.S., certain things stand out. A 30-year, fixed-rate mortgage is one of them. You may take it for granted, but foreigners don't.

Why is it so amazing? Let's take a look at the numbers: When you take out a $136,000 30-year loan, say at a 5% fixed-rate, your monthly payment of principal and interest is approximately $730 a month. I am using a very conservative interest rate of 5%, despite rates for investors being under 3.5% in 2020, since most of the time, rates are not as incredibly low as they are in 2020, partly due to the COVID-19 pandemic, and I want more regular rates to be used in the examples here. You know for a fact that this is going to be the payment for the next 30 years—it will never change. Even if, in 20 years, $730 is barely enough to buy dinner for two, it will still be your mortgage payment.

When I speak in Europe, my audience invariably stops me when I tell them about fixed-rate loans. They think I don't have my facts straight. They think it's not possible. Or they think I'm just plain crazy. They can't comprehend how, in a country where the cost of living keeps rising, banks will lend money for 30 years where the principal and interest payment and the balance of the loan never change—except to go down (in the case of the balance). For anyone outside the U.S., this is truly an unbelievable thing. In other countries, loans are indexed to inflation. It's not inconceivable to get a loan for 136,000 in the local currency where the initial payment is 730 a month, and 12 years later the payment is 1,500 a month, and the balance of the loan is 240,000, despite paying down principal for 12 years. Why? Because the monthly payment and balance of the loan increase to keep up with inflation.

Fixed-rate loans are not just inflation-proof, they're inflation fighters.

We've already seen how the price of everything is steadily going up. Everything except your mortgage balance. That is in fact is going down every month, along with your mortgage payment which, because of inflation, is eroded—it comparatively gets smaller and smaller and smaller all the time.

By financing your investment with a fixed-rate loan, you're actually making money.

 **PAUSE**

Throughout the book, I'll be talking about 30-year, fixed-rate loans, but it's important to keep one thing in mind: you don't have to pay off a 30-year loan in 30 years. You can pay it off whenever you want to—whatever works for your particular financial plan. You can also refinance the original loan to a 15-year note. The advantages of a 30-year loan are it has lower monthly payments, and it's easier to qualify for it. It also allows inflation to erode your loan over a longer period of time. As your investment home increases in value and rental prices rise, you can decide whether to put the profits "in your pocket" or use them to pay off the loan sooner.

Imagine that if in 1980 you had made a deal with Whole Foods (the year it was founded) that you would never have to pay more than 25 cents for a single organic avocado for the next thirty years; after that your organic avocados would be free. Imagine that! In 1990, when everyone else was shelling out 65 cents for an organic avocado, your deal looked pretty good. Now, when an organic avocado might cost two dollars, your deal is even better. And in 10 years when an organic avocado is likely to cost $3.00 or more, your organic avocado will be free! Financially, you will feel fabulous having enjoyed this long-term deal with Whole Foods.

Real Estate Values

When you buy a $170,000 property with only 20% down, and you finance the $136,000 balance with a 30-year, fixed-rate loan, you've done something very powerful for your future.

Why? Because over the long-term (which I define as a minimum of five years, and preferably 10 or more) hard assets, such as real estate, will on average rise in value with the cost of living.

For example, let's say you bought a $170,000 home in an average market, where the property values don't really go up, but just keep pace with inflation. This is called zero real appreciation; however, the value of the home is still increasing 3% per year because of inflation, when inflation is 3% per year.

After one year, your $170,000 home will be worth $175,100. When you had originally put down only $34,000 down to buy the home, that's a 15% return on your investment. (Again, this is somewhat lower when factoring in closing costs, but you get the idea.)

You think that's an imaginary figure? Not at all! Overall, home values appreciate at 1.5 times the rate of inflation, which would bump that $5100 profit up to $7650. And good real estate markets consistently surpass the average.

In the mid-1980s I began investing in Las Vegas—the last property I purchased there was in 1987. In 1990 (only three years later) the market had risen so rapidly that I made a couple of hundred percent return on my investments. (Note: this is based on a 10% down payment, and even some 5% down payment purchases, which was allowed in those days.)

Whether you make a 15% return in one year or a couple of hundred percent return in three years, investing in real estate and holding it for the long term will enable your money to grow at a rate that will consistently outstrip inflation. Revisiting the train metaphor from Chapter 1, once you invest in real estate, you're already staying ahead of the train. And a good market—it doesn't have to be booming, but just going up at a steady pace—will allow you to quickly leave that train in the dust.

But that isn't the only benefit. There's more good news to come.

Financing College Expenses or Retirement

There are two financial planning dilemmas I hear most often.

Scenario One: Tom and Jenny, a younger couple in their thirties, who want to send their newborn daughter to college in 18 years. They know college is already incredibly expensive; they can't even begin to predict what it's going to cost in 18 years. They only know that they can't afford it now, and they don't know how they'll be able to afford it later.

Scenario Two: Marion and Paul, in their fifties, would like to retire in 15 years. They have a 401(k) and an IRA but, even so, they can see that another 15 years of contributions and compounding isn't going to provide them with the kind of wealth they'd like to have. Like most Baby Boomers and Gen X-ers, they don't envision spending their retirement camped out on the couch in front of the TV. They want to travel, play golf and tennis, and set up a trust fund for their kids. What can they do to ensure their retirement lifestyle will be all that they desire?

A Simple Method

Many people get overwhelmed when trying to see 15 or 20 years into the future. Even when you know exactly what you want (and most of us don't; we only know that we want to have enough to maintain our present standard of living), trying to estimate expenses, future financial goals and prepare for the unexpected is simply mind-boggling. Who really knows what the next 15 years will bring, or exactly how much money will be necessary to live comfortably two decades from now?

You might think you need a crystal ball—one that will calculate future earnings, taxes and inflation, and provide a clear vision of what your life will look like in 15 or 20 years.

Happily, a crystal ball isn't required. You don't have to see 20 years into the future. You can estimate your future needs by thinking in today's dollars. I will extend the two previous examples to show you how it's done.

Using Real Estate as a College Fund

Let's start with Tom and Jenny, who wanted to plan for their daughter's college education.

First, what's the cost of attending a four-year university today? As of the 2020-2021 school year, estimates place the combined costs of four years of tuition, housing, and other expenses (based on educationdata. org), at an average of $101,584 for an in-state public school, $170,296 for an out-of-state public school, and $212,408 for a private university. For our example, we'll use $180,000.

What Tom and Jenny needed was an inflation-proof investment. In other words, an investment that would increase in value along with the rising costs of a college education.

I suggested they buy a $170,000 home with $34,000 down and total cash needed (meaning including loan and closing costs) of $41,000. They could finance the remaining $136,000 with a 30-year, fixed-rate loan. However, there's no rule that says you must take 30 years to pay off a 30-year mortgage. Instead of 30 years, I recommended they pay off the loan in 18 years.

How? By making an extra payment on the principal every year. After a few years, their tenants' rent is likely to rise with the cost of living, but their mortgage payment will remain the same. The rental income will make the extra principal payment for them, with the exception of a very small outlay (before tax deductions), in the first year ($60/mo), and a minute outlay ($23/mo) for the 2nd year. After a few more years, the rents are still likely increasing—so not only is the house making the extra principal payment, it's also paying them. For most of those 18 years, the house will be generating profits. After 18 years go by, they'll have a free and clear $170,000 (in today's dollars) home that will cover almost all of the cost of their daughter's $180,000 (in today's dollars) education. Both the home and the college expenses should keep up with the cost of living in a similar manner.

"And if you want to send your daughter to Harvard with a Porsche," I added, "buy two houses."

RENTAL PROPERTY AS COLLEGE FUND

	Year 1	Year 5	Year 10	Year 15	Year 18
Rental Income	$16,800	$19,654	$23,912	$29,092	$31,741
PI + $2,676 Extra Principal	$11,688	$11,688	$11,688	$11,688	$11,688
Tax & Insurance	$2,688*	$3,145	$3,836	$4655	$5,236
Property Mgmt Misc. Expenses Annual Profit/Loss	$1,344 $1,800 $-720	$1,572 $2,106 $1,142	$1,913 $2,371 $4,104	$2,327 $2,774 $7,648	$2,539 $3,120 $9,158
Property Value	$176,800	$206,831	$251,642	$306,160	$344,389
Mortgage Balance	$131,334	$110,020	$76,262	$32,395	$0
Gross Equity	$45,466	$96,811	$175,380	$273,765	$344,389

Using 5.25% fixed 30-year interest rate. PI for 30 years is $751/mo. PI to pay off in 18 years is $974/mo. So, pay an extra $223/mo. ($2,676/yr.) to pay loan off in 18 years. Using Oklahoma City Tax & insurance figures in 2020 for a $170,000 new house.

*The increase in rental income, tax & insurance, property management, misc. expenses, and property value has been calculated using a 4% annual rate. PI = Principal and Interest.

Using Real Estate for Retirement Income

How about Marion and Paul, who wanted to retire in 15 years?

I asked them to estimate the annual income they'd need if they were to retire today. How much would it take for them to live the life of their dreams—now?

They replied that $70,000 per year would cover all their living expenses and financial goals as retirees: travel, trust fund, etc. What Marion and Paul needed was an income that was inflation-proof—one that would continue to generate the equivalent of $70,000 in today's dollars year after year, even 15, 20 or 40 years from now.

Suppose, like Tom and Jenny, they bought a $170,000 home with $34,000 down (approximate total cash needed, including closing costs would be $41,000), and paid off the loan in 15 years. Now it's free and clear, with no mortgage to pay. There are, however, certain expenses that will continue: property tax, insurance, property management, vacancies and repairs. I can tell you from my vast experience of buying thousands of homes that these expenses are going to run approximately $550 a month.

Now, what's the monthly rent on a $170,000 home? Where I live, in the San Francisco Bay Area, there are essentially no single-family homes at this price range in 2020, which is one of the reasons I don't invest there. But there are numerous markets in the U.S. where a $170,000 home rents for approximately $1400 a month. To name just a couple: Oklahoma City, Oklahoma, and Baton Rouge, Louisiana. And for a little more investment upfront, areas like Central Florida, have homes selling for $220,000 and renting for $1,600–$1,700 per month.

If Marion and Paul's house is renting for $1400 each month, and their expenses are $550 each month, that's an $850 profit per month. If one house brings in $850 per month, how many houses will they need to make $5833 per month, or $70,000 per year? Seven. In fact, seven houses will bring in $71,400 per year in this example.

RETIREMENT INCOME from RENTAL PROPERTY				
	Total Income (mo.)	Total Expense (mo.)	Total Profit (mo.)	Total Profit (annual)
1 Rental Property	$1,400	$550	$850	$10,200
2 Rental Property	$2,800	$1,100	$1,700	$20,400
3 Rental Property	$4,200	$1,650	$2,550	$30,600
4 Rental Property	$5,600	$2,200	$3,400	$40,800
5 Rental Property	$7,000	$2,750	$4,250	$51,000
6 Rental Property	$8,400	$3,300	$5,100	$61,200
7 Rental Property	$9,800	$3,850	$5,950	$71,400

One Is Not Enough

Does buying seven houses seem like a far-fetched notion? If you think it is, you're in the majority. Most of us are brought up with a singular goal: to buy our own home. The home you own and live in is probably your biggest asset, yet most of us don't think past our first home purchase... unless it's to trade up to a larger, more expensive house.

In the year 2000, I remember being in New York on my way to give a lecture for The Learning Annex. The cab driver, a friendly fellow in his fifties, asked what I would be lecturing on. When I said real estate, he told me about his house in upstate New York. He'd bought it 25 years before, for only $20,000. It was worth over $525,000 25 years later. He was proud of his investment, for good reason. But I couldn't help thinking what I always think when I hear stories like this (and I hear many), "Why didn't he buy two houses? Or three? He'd be a millionaire now and wouldn't have to drive a cab!"

I know buying even one investment home requires a kind of quantum jump in the way you think about yourself and your future. But to buy seven, or 10, or 15 homes? Only the most experienced real estate investors would do that, right?

Wrong.

Ask any one of the thousands of people—busy people, just like you— whom I've worked with over the past 35 years. None of them are experts, and yet many of them have purchased 5, 10, 15, or 20 homes—or more. The only possible difference between you and them is their financial future is secure. It's a done deal. They don't have to worry about it anymore.

If you are reading this book and live in a place where houses are expensive, the notion of buying more than one home may feel even scarier. Now in 2020, there are a few cities, including some in the San Francisco Bay Area, with median home prices of about $1 million. However, when you buy seven homes for $170,000 each, the total value of all seven homes would be $1,190,000, about the same as the median price for one home in San Francisco. When you think about it in these terms, buying seven homes may not sound very daunting at all.

PAUSE

It isn't necessary to buy all your investment homes at once, of course. You can build your portfolio over time (see Chapter 10 for examples). The main thing is to begin thinking beyond the limited notion that "one is enough," or that "bigger is better."

Investing for the Shorter Term

This is all great, you're thinking, if I wanted to retire in 15 or 20 years, but I'm 57 and I'd like to retire in 10!

What should you do if you've got less time to plan?

To gain the benefits of your investment sooner, you need to use less leverage when buying properties. Putting a down payment of 20%, 30% or 40% will mean a smaller mortgage. The rental income from the property will generate profits immediately—profits you can then use to pay off the mortgage in 10 years.

Back to Marion and Paul

For the couple who wanted to retire in 15 years, I recommended buying seven homes. If the homes average $170,000 each, they need about $34,000 for a 20% down payment, plus about $7000 in closing costs, for a total of $41,000 cash for each property. For seven homes they would need approximately $287,000 in down payments and closing costs. I'm not implying in any way that $287,000 is small change; there's no question it's a lot of money. But look at what it will buy:

- $1,190,000 in real property
- Profits "in your pocket" starting right away (modestly), then increasing constantly and becoming significant within 5 to 10 years
- $71,400 a year in inflation-proof retirement income
- A net worth of $1,190,000, in 15 years, in today's dollars

Now, that's a very solid financial future, but this is only the tip of the iceberg. In addition to providing you with profits, inflation-proof investments/income, and greatly increased net worth, your real estate investments can do something very, very special for you that no other investment type can—something you'll appreciate every time April 15th comes around.

Tax Benefits for Real Estate Investors

In the above examples, I haven't factored in the tax deductions you can take as a real estate investor, which would make the outcome considerably rosier. Most people are aware of the tax breaks homeowners enjoy, but few know investors profit from an even greater number of deductions. If leverage and the 30-year, fixed-rate loan can be considered gifts, then the tax benefits are like a whole bundle from Santa. (For a more complete analysis of tax issues, including further discussion of the new 2018 tax law, please see Chapter 12.)

Just as they are on an owner-occupied home, mortgage interest and real estate taxes are deductible on investment properties. In addition, all repairs are deductible, as are all expenses associated with the property, such as travel and lodging, telephone, and tax preparation. The 2018 tax law also adds a "pass-through deduction" which can further save taxes for most owners of rental homes. However, this may be targeted by the new administration elected in 2020, and may be rescinded in the future.

But that isn't all.

Unlike the home you own and live in, you can depreciate investment property. This is a just-for-tax-purposes, imaginary loss that's calculated over 27.5 years. On a $170,000 property, in a typical metro area we invest in, the tax deduction is approximately $5000 per year. If your adjusted gross income is less than $100,000 per year, you can claim up to $25,000 in these passive losses.

This is the second bit of news that astounds my European audiences.

"You mean to tell me," they say incredulously, "that in the U.S., you can get a fixed-rate loan for 30 years on a piece of property that's going to rise in value, and you can pretend that this same piece of property is declining in value and get a tax break? What kind of country is this?"

You know what I say in reply? "It's a great country."

When we add these tax benefits to the above estimate of what your $287,000 investment will bring, it becomes even more extraordinary.

One Last Thing:
What About the Stock Market?

Personally, I have nothing against the stock market. Done wisely, it's also a good way to invest, and a well-rounded investment portfolio will include, at the very least, some index funds. Over the long term, the stock market also keeps up with or outstrips inflation. But real estate is by its very nature a more stable investment.

Remember leverage? One difference between investing in stocks and real estate is the opportunity to use 1 - 5 leverage when buying property. If you buy $40,000 worth of stock without buying on margin (most people don't buy on margin, because it's dangerous and badly financed), and it goes up 3%, you make $1200. If you buy a $170,000 home with $40,000 down, and it goes up 3%, you make $5100. This leverage will work against you if property values go down, but the whole premise of this book is that you hold your real estate investments for the long term—and in the long term, real estate values have on average risen 1.5 times the rate of inflation, including booms and busts.

REPLAY

- ► Leverage offers the ability to dramatically increase your net worth with a minimum investment.
- ► A 30-year, fixed-rate loan makes money for you, and turns inflation into your ally, as it keeps eroding the real value of your fixed-rate loan.
- ► You can tailor a 30-year loan to meet your financial planning goals by paying it off sooner, in the number of years you choose.
- ► Real estate overall has historically appreciated at 1.5 times the rate of inflation over the long term, even when factoring in occasional booms and busts.
- ► Use real estate as an inflation-proof investment for financial goals, and as inflation-proof income for retirement.
- ► Your own home is probably your greatest asset. Remember you can substantially increase your net worth just by buying one more home!
- ► Think beyond your first purchase: 5, 10 and even 20 homes are within your reach, especially in less expensive markets.
- ► You can build your portfolio over time.
- ► Tax benefits for real estate investors exceed the tax benefits offered to homeowners.

CHAPTER 3

SHORT TERM VERSUS LONG TERM INVESTING

Any time you invest in real estate for the short-term (which I define as five years or less), you take a big risk with your money.

While it's true there's money to be made buying, renovating and selling bargain properties, it's a challenging and time-consuming endeavor..., one that's best left to fulltime real estate experts. Even though real estate outstrips inflation over the long-term, in the short-term, markets will fluctuate. If you purchase an investment property intending to make a profit in less than five years, you're going to be at the mercy of the market—and it has no mercy.

Some people spend an inordinate amount of time charting the ups and downs of real estate markets, hoping to catch a "wave" that will enable them to buy low and sell high. But this is something that no one can predict with total accuracy. The exclusion of just one important factor can send the whole forecast crashing down like a house of cards. How many "seers" foresaw the 1994 debacle in Orange County, California, when one of the most affluent counties in the country declared bankruptcy and sent home prices spiraling downward? How many experts missed the great real estate boom of 2004 through 2006, and the subsequent great recession that affected real estate from 2008 through 2011?

Happily, for busy investors, building wealth with real estate is not contingent upon catching one wave. You don't need to spend your time charting the fluctuations of the market. It's much better—and more lucrative in the long run—to ride the waves and let them take you safely to the farther shore.

A Long-and Short-Term Story

Earlier, I told you about my experience when I entered the workforce and how realized I wanted more to show for my hard work after 15 or 20 years than my colleagues did. Since I grew up in a family of real estate developers, I knew something about real estate. And being very aware of the advantages of investing in real estate in the U.S. it simply made a lot of sense to me.

At first, I started looking around the Bay Area. At the time, (1983-1984), it was possible to buy a decent home in Palo Alto (where Stanford University and Hewlett-Packard are located), for $150,000. These days that seems like an imaginary figures joke, because the current median sold home price in Palo Alto is around $2,800,000 as of 2020, per Realtor.com. Even then, however, that $150,000 house couldn't rent for more than about $700 a month: the discrepancy between the rental income and the mortgage payment was too great. Instead of buying a house in Palo Alto, I bought a house in Sunnyvale and a small apartment building in San Jose. As I looked around for more properties to buy, I realized that if I wanted to keep on investing and make a difference in my future, I couldn't do it in the Bay Area; rents were too low in proportion to the monthly payments.

About a year later, I started buying single-family homes in Las Vegas, Nevada. Las Vegas at that time was a depressed real estate market, and the houses cost about $40,000 each (recall these are mid 1980's numbers). I went about it very aggressively. In my first year and a half, I bought 22 houses.

Many of my engineer friends at Hewlett-Packard, who were logical people, were impressed by what I was doing. Very soon I was leading a group of about 20 friends, all of whom bought investment homes in Las Vegas. We kept on buying there until mid-1987, when the Las Vegas market went up dramatically. The increase in prices was a big bonus for the homes we had already bought, but it wasn't a good time to buy more.

We held on to what we had bought in Las Vegas and started buying in Portland, Oregon. At the time, Portland was a slow real estate market and we bought single- family homes inexpensively..., until Portland, too, started going up.

In 1987, California home prices began to rise rapidly. People were making money hand over fist. As I read the Sunday paper each week, I was astounded by what was happening: price increases of 30% and 35% a year were not uncommon. I owned only a couple of properties in California, so I wasn't benefiting much from the booming market. I decided to stop investing elsewhere and buy houses in the Bay Area, to take advantage of the market's sudden upswing.

I chose to buy in Santa Rosa, about 60 miles north of San Francisco. At the time, it was fairly inexpensive. I began by buying four houses, each for $110,000. I financed them with a 10% down payment (which was allowed as a possible down payment for an investor back in those days) —about $11,000 each plus closing costs. Indeed, they went up to almost $180,000 about a year and a half later, which was an excellent return on my investment.

When I was ready to buy my fifth house, the realtors I worked with connected me with a developer in Santa Rosa who had just finished building an entire sub-division. He had a whole street of unsold homes; he needed to sell and sell fast. So I offered to buy the entire street, and I got a discount, since I was buying in bulk. The average price per home was $99,000. I sold the whole street within ten months, for an average price of $142,000 per home, which means I made a net profit of approximately $30,000 on each.

By the end of 1989, I needed a rest. I decided to go to Hawaii for a whole week and do absolutely nothing except lay on the beach.

Which I proceeded to do quite successfully for about three days. On the fourth day, I found myself in a car with a realtor, looking at houses on Maui. At the time, Hawaii, was a booming market. In Tokyo, you could borrow money very cheaply, almost free, and many people from Japan would come and buy properties for cash—in Hawaii especially and on the mainland as well.

So, I called my friends in the Bay Area and said, "I've just seen a new condo development that I think would be a great investment. There are sixteen units left in phase one, and I think we should buy them all. I think we can sell them quickly to Japanese buyers for cash."

And they said, "We really like your track record and your judgment, but this is the first time you've ever been to Maui, so no thanks."

I bought whatever I could buy as an individual. (When you're from the mainland and you're buying in Hawaii with financing from a Hawaiian lender, and you own more than 10 properties which were all true in my case, you really must put a lot of cash down.) So, I only bought two: one for $305,000, and a second for $250,000. I hired a designer to furnish them for $23,000 apiece. I sold the first one in six weeks for $425,000, and the second went for $394,000 two months later.

It's very nice to go to Hawaii on vacation and make this kind of profit, but since then, when I want to rest I go to Mexico, or the Caribbean Islands, where it's harder to pull off deals like this.

As in Comedy, Timing is Everything

Why am I telling you all this? Three main reasons: first, I want to give you some background; second, I want to brag, and third, it illustrates the difference between short-term and long-term investment.

I've described two types of buying real estate so far. In the first, I bought homes in Las Vegas and other markets as rental properties to be held long-term. In the second, I purchased an entire street and sold it quickly, then "flipped" condos in Maui, and made large profits in a few months. Clearly, the second type of buying sounds a lot more exciting. Who wouldn't want to come back from a vacation a couple of hundred thousand dollars richer?

But when you look at those short-term deals more carefully you'll see that they could have turned out quite differently. When I tell you the story of the condos in Maui, or of the street in Santa Rosa, they sound perfect. They are perfect, because they're finished. But suppose that I was speaking to you right now and said, "You know, I was just in Maui last week, and there are condos, we should buy them, come on, let's go, let's do it."

You'd say, "Hold on a minute. How can you be sure that you can sell them quickly for a profit?" You'd be absolutely right to be so cautious. More than anything else, it was luck and timing that made those deals happen.

I closed escrow on the Hawaiian condos in January 1989. The first one sold in April 1989, and the second one in June, two months later. Guess what? In the summer of 1989, the Hawaiian real estate market tumbled—absolutely crashed.

If I had taken my vacation a little bit later, or if the condos hadn't sold so soon, I would have been stuck with two vacation rentals, with a lot of my cash tied up in them and a negative cash flow. The Hawaiian market went down so much that the condos' value was soon less than the loans I had taken out.

I was lucky. What about the street in Santa Rosa that I bought and sold? Same thing. I started buying in Santa Rosa in January of 1988. By the time I purchased the street it was mid-1988. I closed a few months later, closing escrow in July, which means I finished selling the street just around May of 1989.

In May of 1989, the California market started to slow down. If the deal in Santa Rosa had closed a few months later than it did, I would've lost a lot of money and been stuck with a whole street of homes that were declining in value.

As it stood, I made a lot of money on both of those deals, but it was nothing but luck and timing. And that's always the case. Whenever you want to speculate and make a quick buck in real estate, you're taking a risk. You're hoping it will happen, but you had better be financially prepared to hold on to the property for the long-term, just in case.

I had a similar story later, when I bought 16 condos in Las Vegas in 2004 for a very good price. Since in 2005 and 2006 there was a big price boom in many states (including Nevada), I sold some of the units for a good profit. However, I left about two thirds of them, and during the recession they went down so much, they were severely "underwater" (the loans balances were far higher than the property values). The remaining ones nearly were lost to foreclosure. This is one case where you can see the effect of timing: for the first few units, it worked out, for the ones that remained—timing turned the deal into a disaster.

The Four Conditions of Flipping Properties

"Flipping" a property means selling it soon after you purchase it. The intention, of course, is to make a quick profit.

As I said earlier, quick profits in real estate rely too much on luck and timing to be a dependable source of income. It's not investing, it's gambling.

The real estate "gurus" who extol the virtues of flipping properties make it sound simple; too simple, in fact. According to them, anyone can find a bargain property and sell it quickly for a profit. This strategy sounds reasonable, but when you examine it more carefully, you discover it's as full of holes as a slice of Swiss cheese. To successfully flip a property, four essential conditions are required: you must buy below market value; the market must should preferably keep rising, or at least not go down; you must find a buyer who will pay full price; and your profits must exceed your actual costs. Let's look at these elements one at a time:

You've Just Purchased a Bargain Property.

What exactly makes a property a "bargain"?" By definition, a bargain property has an appraised or estimated value above what you paid for it (, i.e., a single family home appraised at $200,000 that you purchase for $160,000). The catch is this: if no one is offering to pay $200,000, then the property is not actually worth $200,000. (And if they are, your $160,000 bid will be ignored.)

No matter what the appraised or estimated value of a property, its actual worth is based on what the seller can get for it. If you purchase a "$200,000 property" for $160,000, you've just bought a property worth—guess what?—$160,000.

The Market Will Keep Rising in the Short Term.

As illustrated above, even booming markets can suddenly stop booming— and even plummet. If short-term market fluctuations were predictable, then few people would ever lose money on real estate.

But markets are not entirely predictable in the short term. In order to sell your property quickly for a profit, the market must rise.

You'll Find a Buyer Who Will Pay Full Price.

If you weren't willing to pay more than $160,000 for the property, how can you be certain that, in a month or two, you'll find a buyer willing to pay $200,000 or more?

If the market is rising very rapidly, this may happen. Otherwise, you're relying on the "bigger fool" theory: that someone with limited knowledge of local real estate values will pay an inflated price for your property.

Profits Will Exceed Your Actual Costs.

Let's assume that you could sell your $160,000 property in three months for $200,000. How much money have you made?

First, you must deduct the down payment (20%, or $32,000); closing costs and lender's fees for a $128,000 loan; realtor commissions when you sell; mortgage payments until the property sells (let's assume you can sell it in three months, a fairly quick turn-around); and any costs associated with repairing and showing the property. (Let's suppose that it isn't a fixer-upper, but just needed some cleaning up and a bit of landscaping.) And, of course, you must pay taxes on your profits. So, what's the rough bottom line?

GROSS PROFIT:	**$40,000**	
Closing & loan costs on purchase:		($6,000)
Commissions & closing costs on sale:		($14,000)
Mortgage payments:		($2,800)
Painting, cleaning, repairs, landscaping:		($6,000)
Misc. expenses:		($1,000)
NET PROFIT:	**$10,200**	
Less Ordinary Income Federal income tax (32% tax bracket)		($3,264)
AFTER TAX PROFIT:	**$6,936**	

In my opinion, that isn't much to show for the time, money and effort involved in finding this example "bargain" property", making cosmetic improvements, and putting it back on the market. And yet, the selling price of $200,000 represents a 25% increase over the purchase price of $160,000—an enormous jump for only three months.

Long-Term Investing

As illustrated by the chart on the next page, real estate really shows its power over the long term. The figures in the chart represent an investment in a $180,000 property, with a 20% down payment and the remaining $144,000 financed with a 5% 30-year fixed-rate mortgage. As of this writing, at the end of 2020, investor rates are about 3.4%. However, these rates are exceedingly low, and partly a result of the COVID-19 pandemic. I am using 5%—which is still a low rate historically—throughout this book, as I would like the usefulness of these calculations to extend for a long time, beyond the current ultra-low rates.

Line one shows rental income starting at $18,000 per year and rising 3% per year. Line two shows how principal and interest payments remain the same. Line three shows a 3% rise in tax and insurance each year (these figures are based on property tax rates for the state of Oklahoma; some states may be lower or higher).

The fourth and fifth lines of the chart reveal how profits and property values become very powerful over the long term. Most importantly, the mortgage balance decreases as rental income and property value rise. I've calculated the increase in property value at 3% per year— a conservative figure for many markets. And yet you can see that with only an under-investment of less than $40,000 investment (20% down payment plus loan & closing costs), in 20 years this property will be generating nearly $16,000 per year in profit and have a value of $325,000 with over quarter million dollars of gross equity. If the home prices were to appreciate at an average rate of 4% (which is still historically a low average), the value in 20 years would be $394,402 and the gross equity would be $321,518. At 5% per year average price appreciation, the value in 20 years would be $477,593 and the gross equity $404,709—over $400,000 on an initial $40,000 investment.

LONG TERM INVESTMENT PROFITS

	Year 1	Year 5	Year 10	Year 15	Year 20
Rental Income	$18,000	$20,867	$24,190	$28,043	$32,510
Principal & Interest	$9,276	$9,276	$9,276	$9,276	$9,276
Tax & Insurance	$2,740[*]	$3,176	$3,682	$4,269	$4,949
Property Mgmt Fees	$1,440	$1,669	$1,935	$2,243	$2,600
Annual Profit	$4,544	$6,746	$9,297	$12,255	$15,685
Property Value	$185,400	$208,669	$241,905	$280,434	$325,100
Mortgage Balance	$141,876	$132,234	$117,133	$97,754	$72,884
Gross Equity	$43,524	$76,435	$124,772	$182,680	$252,216

The increase in rental income, tax & insurance, property management and property value has been calculated using a 3% annual rate (I use a 3% rate in this example and have used 4% in another example. This is to illustrate that these are merely examples, and the rate can vary.) For simplicity, HOA (if any) and unexpected costs (repairs/vacancy), were not calculated in this example.

**REPLAY**

- ► Properly buying, renovating and selling properties is usually a full-time job better done by professionals.
- ► In the short-term, markets fluctuate. Over the long-term, they steadily go up, rising, historically on average 1.5 times the cost of living.
- ► You don't have to chart the markets, just stay in for the long-term.
- ► Short-term profits rely on luck and timing.
- ► Even if you speculate, you must be prepared to hold on to the property for the long-term.
- ► Real estate really shows its power over the long-term.

CHAPTER 4

WHAT TO BUY

Most real estate books present an overview of the types of real estate in which you can invest, from small apartment buildings and condos to commercial real estate and undeveloped land. I'm not going to do that. I've tried just about every kind of real estate investment there is, and there's only one that works for the busy investor: the single-family home.

A True American Dream

Single-family homes are the stuff of which the American Dream is made. Everyone wants the picket fence, the yard, and the two-car garage. More than any other type of real estate, single-family homes are always in demand, and are therefore the most liquid. When the market goes up, single-family homes sometimes go up first and most, as their price is driven as much by emotion as by cold numbers. When the market goes down, single-family homes have been shown to go down last and least (although they behaved differently during the recession that started in 2008). As an investment, they're the most stable; as a piece of property, they're the easiest to rent, maintain, manage and sell. For busy investors, quality single-family homes located in good neighborhoods offer the most effortless, stress-free real estate investment possible, with the best appreciation potential.

Single-family homes are the best investment in terms of liquidity, financing, ease of management and appreciation. I know this from personal experience. Single-family homes generate the financial benefits that will secure your future without the hassles many other types of property entail. However, I stress this: the only kind of single-family homes to buy are quality single-family homes, located in good neighborhoods.

What do I mean by "quality" single-family homes?

I mean a house that's new, or reasonably new, and in good structural condition. One that's aesthetically appealing, has a well-tended, functional yard, a garage, two baths, and at least three bedrooms. It doesn't have to be a showplace or the house of your dreams—in fact, it probably shouldn't be. But it should be a place where a local family can live comfortably.

Don't Confuse Cash Flow with Quality

If quality single-family homes are such a great investment, you may be wondering, why haven't other books told you the same thing?

**PAUSE**

The Top Five Reasons to Buy Single-Family Homes

1. Financing is best for single-family homes (technically 1-4 residential units).

2. Single-family homes are easiest to rent, manage, maintain and sell.

3. Single-family homes attract stable tenants.

4. Single-family homes are more liquid than other types of real estate.

5. Single-family homes are most appropriate for "real people" (not just wealthier or very experienced investors).

For one, buying a single-family home isn't the most exciting investment. It doesn't have the same caché as, for instance, purchasing an apartment complex or a mini-mall. But along with bragging rights go a lot of headaches. I've tried those other kinds of investments, yet I've made the most (and easiest) money with single- family homes; the least "macho" real estate.

Do I care? Not at all.

At first glance, quality single-family homes have the worst cash flow. When you look at older, lower-quality single-family homes in matching neighborhoods, their cash flow seems better: as an example, a $75,000 house that rents for $900 is more profitable (on paper) than a $170,000 house that rents for $1400. So why do I continue to recommend quality single-family homes?

Because cash flow on paper doesn't tell the whole story. Older, low-quality properties require more repairs, and often encounter frequent tenant turn-over. These not only cost you money, but time. In addition, a low-quality home won't appreciate as rapidly as a high-quality home.

Quality single-family homes attract good, stable tenants who pay their rent on time and don't damage your property—and that's what's going to help make your investment work. Remember, you're investing for the long-term. A quality single-family home will continue to rise in value, and your rental income will increase with the cost of living.

When you look at the big picture, you'll see that even a property starting out with a negative cash flow can soon become positive. Of course, in 2020, with the interest rates around 3.4% on a 30-year fixed rate loans for investors, most properties are likely to have a positive cash flow from the get-go. You can't talk about cash flow without talking about cash flow after taxes. This is one time that Uncle Sam is giving money to you. As I mentioned earlier, I will use 5% for the calculations in this book, since 3.4% is exceptionally low, and is the result of lowering interest rates in the extreme due to the 2020 COVID-19 pandemic. 5% is still a low rate historically, and likely a bit into the future, post-pandemic.

$170,000 SINGLE-FAMILY HOME 5-YEAR CASH FLOW FIGURES					
	Year 1	Year 2	Year 3	Year 4	Year 5
Rental Income	$16,800	$17,304	$17,823	$18,358	$18,909
Principal & Interest	$8,761	$8,761	$8,761	$8,761	$8,761
Tax & Insurance	$2,620	$2,688	$2,769	$2,852	$2,938
Misc. Expenses	$1,500	$1,545	$1,591	$1,639	$1,688
Gross Profit (Loss)	$3,919	$4,310	$4,702	$5,106	$5,522
Depreciation Deduction	$4,945	$4,945	$4,945	$4,945	$4,945
Net Profit	$3,919	$4,310	$4,702	$5,098	$5,337

In the example shown above, first year figures show a before-tax profit of $3,919. After adding in tax savings from the depreciation deduction, the property shows a net profit of $3,919, as the depreciation more than covered the profit (in fact there is a small additional loss remaining which can be used elsewhere). Each year, as rental rates increase, positive cash flow also increases.

The Hidden Costs of Small Apartment Buildings

Of course, there are other types of real estate you can invest in which can work successfully—for example, large apartment complexes of over 100 units, or shopping malls. But by virtue of their cost, these kinds of real estate investments are available only to wealthier, experienced investors, or to syndications and corporations, etc.—not to the average person.

You may have read books that suggest buying a small apartment building—say four to ten units—as your first investment. The authors' main reason for this is that apartment buildings can generate positive cash flow.

It's often true that, on paper, small apartment buildings can seem like a dream come true. They can be a nightmare. The same authors who tell you to buy apartments will also tell you that managing them is a piece of cake, and dealing with numerous tenants, repairs, etc., is a small price to pay for the all-important cash flow. But I can tell you this isn't so: managing apartment buildings is more demanding than managing single-family homes. For the busy investor who wants to have a life outside of real estate, small apartment buildings can be a sure path to ulcers and migraines...even bankruptcy and divorce.

To illustrate, let me tell you a story about a fourplex I bought in Albuquerque, New Mexico. Here's what it looked like on paper (the price is from the recession of the beginning of the 1990s and this 4-plex was bought from the Farmers' Home Administration as an REO after foreclosure):

FOURPLEX CASH FLOW FIGURES	
Purchase Price:	$27,000
10% Down:	$2,700
Mortgage:	$24,300
PITI:	$400 per month
Rental Income:	$1,200 per month
Gross Profit:	$800 per month

It seems like an excellent deal, yes? Unfortunately, no. Here's what happened in real life:

I bought the fourplex in foreclosure from the government for only $2,700 down. Each unit rented for $300 a month. That's a $1,200 monthly income against a $400 per month PITI (principal, interest, taxes and insurance). With an $800 per month profit, it sounds like a great investment. But the fourplex never had a positive cash flow. There were many fourplexes in the area, so often at least one of my units was vacant. Many tenants didn't pay rent or damaged the property. It was constantly being repaired. I sold it for less than what I had paid for it and felt lucky to get out before it gobbled up any more cash.

Small apartment buildings can have "hidden" costs that don't show up in the initial numbers. Not to mention the price you pay with your sanity.

I have had other experiences with larger properties—from an 88-unit complex (not enough units to get good economies of scale), to 110 units and more. Despite using property managers, the owner of an apartment complex needs to run it like a business since that's really what it is —a business! Getting into this field without a lot of experience can cause large losses. Of course, professional, usually full-time, apartment complex specialists can make it work (and well). However, for the individual investor, especially one busy with other things, I do not recommend this path.

I'll repeat: don't confuse cash flow with quality. Remember, you're investing for the long-term.

The Truth About Foreclosures

Bargain properties, such as foreclosures, are the classic real estate lure. Now, I like a sale as much as the next guy. Who wouldn't want to buy a $180,000 house (for example) for only $110,000? That sounds great! Go to a couple of popular real estate seminars and you'll see foreclosure fever in action. Instant wealth! Overnight success! And where does it all come from? Foreclosures! Listen long enough, and you'll get the impression that buying foreclosures is as easy as plucking ripe berries from a vine. But if you dive into the foreclosure field's thorny brambles, you may find that instead of plucking, you're the one who's getting...plucked.

You have to think logically. There are many people out there who specialize in foreclosure deals. A good number of them are making a living at it, and some of them are doing very well. However, these people are professionals who buy foreclosures full-time. Now, suppose they work in the same town where you're trying to buy foreclosures. Doesn't it stand to reason that if there's a good deal out there, they'll get to it long before you do? Of course, they will! So, what's left over for you, the busy, part-time investor?

I'll tell you what's left over: the junk no one else wants. You must be really careful. It's too easy for more experienced people to manipulate and sway you. For instance, a seller could have a lousy property he's dying to get rid of, but he's not giving it back to the bank or walking away from it because he doesn't want to ruin his credit. But he could lure you, the unsuspecting investor who just bought a home-study course on buying foreclosures, with his "bargain" price and offer to give you $3,000 at the close of escrow. And you think, "Wow! These courses work!"

You know what the seller thinks? "What a sucker! I've been trying to get this white elephant off my hands for two years!" The pros are always going to beat you to the best stuff.

You'll get the leftovers. And, unfortunately, you'll be competing for those leftovers with lots of other people who are looking for foreclosures part-time. Doing this part-time can expose you to giant risks.

Even when a foreclosure deal appears to be easy and readily available, it may not be your best bet. I know this from experience. I have purchased dozens of VA (Veterans Administration) repossessed properties (repos) in various states. On the surface, these REOs (REO stands for "Real Estate Owned" and is the term commonly used when a lending institution forecloses on a property) seemed like great deals. Typically, they were sold by the VA for no money down or an extremely low down payment, such as $1000. In the case of the no-money-down sales, the VA itself gave the buyer a 100% loan on the property—a 30-year, fixed-rate loan at very attractive rates.

What could be more perfect, right? After analyzing what I had bought, however, I realized that buying beautiful, brand new homes at market value from a builder was a much better deal.

Here's why: the great financing and no-money-down terms were so enticing, many buyers greatly overbid the properties so many sold at well over market value—not a great start! (Buyers submitted their bids for the

REOs in sealed envelopes and the highest bidder "won.") The VA charged two loan points (2% of the loan); along with the other closing expenses—making the total cost for the purchase about 4% of the property value. In addition, the REOs were sold in as-is condition, and many of them had been vacant and boarded up for months prior to the sale. It took, on average, about 6% of the property's price to fix it up and bring it up to rental standard. The REOs also sold with the utilities turned off, and they could not be turned on until after the sale had taken place. In some cases, there plumbing or electrical systems came with nasty surprises. Repairing those systems cost, on average, another 1.5% of the property price.

All in all, this "no-money-down" REO deal had an average cost of 10% to 11.5% of the property's price—and that's to buy an older, overpriced property in a neighborhood that, more often than not, the buyer didn't choose (and often wasn't a good neighborhood).

If, instead, I had bought a brand new property at market value, in a great part of town, the initial costs would have been about the same at that time (when down payments were routinely 10%), the price in many cases would have been better, and usually the condition of the property (as well as the neighborhood) would have been infinitely better.

All in all, the brand new home would have made a far better real estate deal—and with no effort at all! The inferior REO deal required hunting, bidding, and repairing—lots of work—for a worse deal!

Of course, we bought many REOs and other foreclosed properties during the recession between 2008 and 2011. This was an appropriate time to do so, due to the extreme price drops and the massive wave of foreclosures that engulfed many states. This time frame was an exception to the rule, and fitting for buying foreclosures. However now, in 2020, it is a "regular" time: no boom (besides the price escalation during the COVID-19 pandemic, which made single-family homes more desirable than they usually are, due to safe social distancing, a yard, and room for a home office), no bust. During regular times it is highly recommended to invest in brand new (if possible) single- family homes in good areas. Over time, those have created the highest overall yield with the least amount of effort.

Unless you're a real estate expert, foreclosures can waste a lot of your time and money—but the whole point of Remote Controlled Real Estate Riches is you don't need to be an expert to make great real estate investments.

After all, wouldn't you rather be playing golf than looking for termites?

On Airbnb and Vacation Rentals

From time to time, an investor asks me about investing in a short-term vacation rental, or using a property in a central location as an Airbnb rental. On paper, this may seem like an attractive proposition. The calculated numbers on paper may seem enticing. Many of these aspiring short-term owners have a limited scope of time. They forget what happened in 2008-2011, and certainly in recessions past. During a recession, vacation rentals dry up, hotel occupancy plummets, and Airbnb properties tend to stay vacant a lot more. What looks attractive on paper now may be a formula for losing a property to foreclosure during a future recession.

During the COVID-19 pandemic, Airbnb properties were some of the first casualties, standing vacant as travel stopped almost entirely, while single-family homes thrived—see more ahead. By contrast, single-family homes in big city suburbs, typically rented to families with kids, don't display such a drop-off during a recession. We have discussed in a previous newsletter, that during a recession, single-family home rental rates are actually BETTER, since would-be home-buyers are scared to buy and remain as renters. These homes are not short-term rentals. These are not vacation rentals. These are long term rentals of homes rented to families, typically with kids who go to school. These families need a place to live.

Since these are not vacation rentals, recessions do not leave them empty. It's a very important lesson to learn, with the perspective of looking back at how vacation and short-term rentals perform during downturns. I think that buying regular single-family homes and renting them to families is a tried and true strategy to building stable and strong future wealth. There are other issues with Airbnb properties such as liability, insurance issues, and other dangers. Not too long ago, there was a shooting at a party at an Airbnb rental in the San Francisco Bay Area. The lawsuits are just starting to form. If the owners didn't have commercial insurance covering short term rentals, they may lose more than just the home. With single-family homes rented long term, insurance is standard and the issues are clear. As always, investors seek the buzzwords.

Over the history of investing in rental homes, some of the favorite buzzwords were: "no money down", "motivated seller", "flip", "Airbnb", and many others. These buzzwords make investments sound a lot sexier than the simple, almost boring act of buying a brand-new home in a good area—a large metro area in the sunbelt—and financing it with a fixed rate 30-year loan. Once the home has been bought, a local management firm leases it for you. Your job is then to do nothing, while letting inflation erode your fixed debt, while the tenants gradually pay off the loan. This is simple, powerful and time-tested way to get wealthy over the long term.

As I said previously, During the COVID-19 pandemic, which first created shelter-in-place orders in parts of the U.S. in March of 2020, the short-term effect on vacation rentals was devastating. Airline travel plummeted, and most people were not traveling. The sector which felt the harshest economic impact was the vacation rental sector.

Single-family homes actually became more in-demand, since they provide safe social distancing, a yard, and potentially more room for a home office, as large groups of employees transitioned to working from home. The low interest rates during the pandemic increased demand for property, mostly single-family homes around the U.S.

Even when travel resumed partially, and with some increased activity of Airbnb homes serving as getaways, they didn't hold a candle to the steady performance of single-family homes.

Beware of the Motivated Seller

What does it mean when a seller is "motivated"? It means he has a house he can't get rid of or needs to sell so quickly he's willing to discount the price or offer concessions. In some instances, the motivated seller may loan you the down payment, and carry back a second mortgage. This can help you purchase a home, I'll admit. But do you have time to look for these motivated sellers? For busy investors, motivated sellers are even harder to find than fast profits from foreclosures.

Too often, the truth behind the veil of a motivated seller is the property is not a good investment. If it wasn't a good investment for him, it probably won't be for you. In short: you're likely buying a bad property. Because if it wasn't a bad property, someone else would buy it for the full price and the seller wouldn't be "motivated" to make all those concessions.

Quality properties in good markets usually don't have motivated sellers. And I only recommend buying in good markets. What are good markets? That's the subject of the next chapter.

REPLAY

- ► Single-family homes are the best investment for the individual investor in terms of:
  - • liquidity,
  - • financing,
  - • ease of management and appreciation.
- ► Quality single-family homes are best for long-term investments.
- ► Don't confuse cash flow with quality.
- ► Even a property that starts out with a negative cash flow can soon become positive. Although in 2018, with the low interest rates, most properties start out with a positive cash flow.
- ► Remember to include tax benefits into cash flow figures.
- ► Small apartment buildings can have hidden costs.
- ► Foreclosures are risky for part-time, busy investors.
- ► Beware of the motivated seller.

CHAPTER 5

WHERE TO BUY

Many novice real estate investors are told to "invest only within a 30-minute drive of where you live." In high-priced markets this doesn't make sense. When the mortgage payment on an investment property greatly exceeds the rent one can expect as income, there's no point to investing. If you follow the 30-minute rule, you may have to wait years before the market in which you live becomes viable. Looking nationally, there's always an appropriate market in which to invest.

There are numerous markets in the U.S. where quality homes in good neighborhoods can be purchased for less than $200,000 and produce a break-even or positive cash flow right from the start, despite using high leverage. In this age of email, overnight mail and social media, we can (much to the horror of the old sages) expand our horizons well beyond the 30-minute boundary and buy rental property nationwide.

The Five Essential Criteria of a Good Market

You've heard the adage of "location, location, location"—and for good reason. Buying in a good market is a kind of insurance policy for your investment.

What is a good market? From decades of investing in properties across the U.S., I've distilled the main features of a good market down to five.

 **PAUSE**

The Five Features of a Good Market

1. Big City

2. Good Rental Market Where the Numbers Work

3. Not a Booming Market

4. Low Median Price

5. Sun Belt States

Big City

A big city has economic diversity that ensures stability. In a small town, there might be only one source of employment, and if it goes out of business the rental market is ruined. In addition, a big city offers numerous property management firms. This means property managers are more competitive (with better services and rates).

When I say, "Big City", I refer specifically to the entire metropolitan area surrounding a city. In fact, the suburbs surrounding the city itself are usually the best, as families live there who likely have kids who will be going to school, creating a stable rental experience.

A Good Rental Market Where the Numbers Work

A good market has single-family homes that rent at a certain percentage of their value; generally, where a $200,000 home will rent for $1,600 a month, and a \$170,000 home will rent for \$1,400 or so. Of course, these ratios look different when comparing markets with high property taxes and insurance, and markets with low property taxes and/or insurance, but you get the general idea.

Not a Booming Market

A booming market is not where you want to invest. By "booming," I don't just mean prices are rising rapidly. Booming implies there are numerous offers for each property; and a frantic public mindset, in which people feel they must buy immediately...before home prices rise higher. In a booming market you'll have to compete with many other buyers and may not get the best price for the home. It's okay to buy in a market where prices are steadily going up, but not one in which prices are escalating rapidly.

Low Median Price

High-priced markets such as San Francisco and Los Angeles are generally not good places to buy (again, the 2008-2011 recession was an exception). First, the numbers don't work: the rental prices are too low in comparison with the monthly mortgage payments. And second, expensive homes require jumbo loans. In San Francisco circa 2021, a jumbo loan is one above \$822,375. To secure a jumbo loan as an investor (not owner-occupier), you usually need a 25% down payment (this can vary based on individual lenders). In other words, a \$1,050,000 property would require a minimum down payment of \$262,500—a rather large chunk of change for the average investor, in addition to loan and closing costs. A good market will have a median home price of about \$160,000 to \$260,000 or so.

Sun Belt

The recent census shows the Sun Belt is the fastest growing region of the country. Its warm weather and lower housing costs make it very attractive to retirees. As Baby Boomers continue to retire, we can expect the Sun Belt to grow even more.

The retirees of today (and even more so in the future) will likely be quite different from those of the past. They'll travel and play sports.

They'll eat out often and attend cultural events. Tomorrow's retirees will insist upon a broad range of activities and will create jobs in the areas they settle. In addition, we already see many Baby Boomer retirees starting new ventures, businesses, and becoming entrepreneurs in retirement. All of this indicates economic stability and long-term growth. Buying in Sun Belt markets will help ensure your investment will continue to grow over the long-term.

In addition, most Sun Belt states have a strong pro-business attitude with less taxation and are inviting the relocation of major companies. They also have landlord-tenant laws that don't heavily favor the tenant. If it becomes necessary to evict a tenant, you'll find it can be done expeditiously—unlike in California or New York, where a knowledgeable tenant can reside at your property without paying rent for up to one year.

The Best Markets in the U.S.

Now that you know the criteria, you may be wondering if it exists. In fact, there are currently some cities in the U.S. with all the above features.

During the boom of 2004-2006, many of the good Sun Belt markets had a very strong price appreciation. These were markets like Phoenix, Las Vegas, Orlando, Jacksonville, Tampa, and others, including the metropolitan areas in California. Some cities had home values double during that time. Fast price appreciation (which was not accompanied by much rent appreciation), rendered these markets unfit for buyers, but great for sellers (Sellers' Markets).

During the subsequent recession (which had a strong downward effect on these same markets between 2008 and 2011), the prices in these markets tanked very rapidly, sometimes by as much as 70% or more. Of course, during and immediately following the Great Recession, these same large Sun Belt metropolitan areas became excellent places for buyers to purchase homes (Buyers' Markets).

In the aftermath, however, these cities rebounded greatly from 2012 until 2020 (so far); in many cases outstripping the values of the 2006 peak. At the same time, rents went up at a much slower clip, rendering many of the classical Sun Belt cities unfit for buyers (and pretty good places to be a seller).

Thus in 2020, Phoenix and Las Vegas are priced too high, with rents not sufficiently covering mortgage payments. These two markets are fit for sellers: home prices in both Phoenix and Las Vegas more than doubled during those eight years.

In Florida the picture is a bit different; while prices did rebound very significantly since 2012, they did not go as high as the prices in cities in Arizona, Nevada, or even California. One reason is the judicial foreclosure process in Florida (meaning it goes through the courts). Not surprisingly, during the recession the Florida courts buckled under the immense load of many thousands of foreclosures, and the length of time to foreclose has become very long (years, instead of several months as in Arizona and other states). As a result, even years after the recession, foreclosed homes still hit the market (being sold by the banks who had taken them back), depressing the full extent of the price recovery. **Therefore, despite good price appreciation, even in 2020 there are areas in Florida which could still be looked at by a buyer**.

In 2013, investors realized much of the discount created by the Great Recession was no longer available. Investors started looking at new markets to invest in, and since the recession left scars, investors put a premium on stable markets which did not violently ride the roller coaster (the upswings of 2004-2006 followed by the downswings of 2008-2011).

Two states stood out as relatively stable: Texas and Oklahoma. In 2013 I told investors if they examine Dallas and Oklahoma City (which are close geographically), I would recommend buying in Oklahoma City over Dallas since the home prices were similar at the time. The rents were also similar, yet the property taxes in Oklahoma City are about 2.5 times less than those in Dallas, hence leading to better cash flow.

Of course, most people went for the more famous name "Dallas" (hey, there was a TV series named after it!) and indeed, Dallas (as well as Austin) home prices shot up by about 60% or more from 2013 until 2020. As a result, in 2020, Oklahoma City looks more appropriate for the savvy investor: the prices are substantially less than those in Dallas, the rents are a little less, and the property taxes are still about two and a half times less. In addition, huge oil and gas reserves were discovered near Oklahoma City, creating a potential for a future boom (despite the clean energy initiatives, oil and gas are likely to continue to be in demand, not only in parts of the U.S, but in large countries like India and China for the foreseeable future). For the reader who says "Well, I should have bought in Dallas in 2013 and enjoyed the appreciation," the response is that no one knows the future. Speculating in the hope of short term price appreciation usually proves futile, and it's so easy to be a "Monday Morning Quarterback." The question to ask is: What is the best place to buy in NOW, based on solid fundamentals. In fact, you might want to watch out not using "well I missed that boom. I shouldn't do anything now," as yet another reason to derail your steady progress.

I get many calls from investors interested in buying in various cities and want my opinion.

One of the popular markets right now (2020) is the Austin metro area. People get excited about the Apple campus expansion and the overall thriving of the local high-tech scene. It is tempting to think of Austin as a good destination to buy in 2020. However, it is not! Austin, in fact, is a good city to be a SELLER in 2020. The Austin prices have climbed rapidly in the past seven years, while rents went up much more slowly. As a result, the rents are too low to cover all expenses.

One expense in Austin (and in the state of Texas overall) is the very high property taxes. The property taxes in Austin can get to almost 3% of the home value per year. That is over 2.5% the property tax rate in Oklahoma (or California). Together, the high prices, relatively low rents (relative to the prices, that is), and the high property taxes, as well as high insurance costs, create an untenable cash flow.

It is very tempting for a California resident to say, "What? I can buy a new home in Austin for 'only' $280,000? That is so cheap!" Yes, it is "cheap" relative to San Francisco prices. However, it is not cheap to buy, and has weak cash flow.

Austin is a place where many of our savvy investors are now SELLING, as the selling market is relatively strong. It is not uncommon to see an investor selling one Austin home and buying three brand new homes via a 1031 tax-deferred exchange in Oklahoma City, or Tulsa, or Baton Rouge, or Central Florida. This move creates much more quality real estate owned, more 30-year fixed-rate loans at today's low rates, and brand new properties with brand new roofs, air conditioners, etc.

Similar logic applies to the Dallas Ft. Worth metro area (DFW), Houston, Phoenix and Las Vegas, which I mentioned above, Nashville and others. Some misguided reporters writing in newspaper articles, confuse high prices and growth with an attractive place to invest in. The two are not necessarily linked. Finally, even when a market is up, (but still not excessively so) it may be viable, as is the case with the Raleigh-Durham area.

If you've got the time, you could do lots of research and possibly discover a few more. Based on our research, the (relatively few) markets where buying makes sense in 2020 (and of course, the list is likely to change somewhat in the future) are:

THE BEST U.S. REAL ESTATE INVESTMENT MARKETS
circa 2018:

Oklahoma City, OK

Baton Rouge, LA

Orlando/Tampa Corridor, FL North, East & South of Orlando

Tulsa, OK

Raleigh Durham, NC (getting expensive but still works)

Parts of Atlanta, GA

The Paralysis of Over-Analysis

People find all sorts of reasons for not investing in real estate. One is the fear that, unless they make a "perfect" deal, one in which all the elements are just right, it won't work, and they'll lose their shirt.

But a deal doesn't have to be the deal of the century for it to work for you. For example, an investor I know called me up in 2000 (when some of the best markets to buy were Phoenix and Las Vegas) and said, "I read an article in the newspaper yesterday that said Naples, Florida was the best market in the country. I don't want to buy in Phoenix and Orlando any more...just Naples."

First, what suddenly turned Naples into the best market in the country? It had shot up dramatically in the previous year, which meant it was no longer a great place to buy. He was shooting himself in the foot!

Just recently, I had a similar discussion with an investor who read "Austin is the place." The writer of the article was impressed with how fast prices in Austin went up, not considering that this is what made Austin a market that is not appropriate to buy in at this time (precisely because the prices became too high, while rents lagged behind, as I discussed previously).

With the advent of blogs, vlogs, and the ability of almost everyone to write and appear very professional and reach a large audience, it is important to remember that sometimes a blog, opinion piece, or short video can be based on a completely wrong idea and mislead the audience into thinking these are bible-worthy opinions, rather than the opinion of a newbie investor.

Second, who cares about the article? Next week there will be an article about Dallas...and the week after that, Albuquerque.

Trying to keep tabs on the "best" market in the country could become a big waste of your time. It is more important to find a good market, buy there, and stay there for as long as makes financial sense. When people ask me, "What's the best market in the country?" I always answer, "It's infinitely better to buy a house in the third best market in the country than not to buy a house in the best market in the country."

Just do it, already! You can't enjoy the benefits of real estate if you don't own real estate. It always surprises me how many people fall into the trap of doing nothing. I call it the "paralysis of over-analysis."

They buy books, and go to seminars and bootcamps —but they never buy properties.

Don't make yourself crazy looking for the Holy Grail. Just remember the five essential criteria, then spend your weekends having some fun.

PAUSE

Five Main Features of a Good Neighborhood

1. Safe
2. Good schools (don't think they need to be GREAT schools!)
3. Convenient shopping
4. Majority of homes owned by residents
5. Composed primarily of single-family homes

Breaking the 30-Minute Rule

When people consider buying an investment home out of town or even out of state, they have a lot of questions: Isn't it risky? How will I check on the property? How will I handle repairs and maintenance? What if the house doesn't rent? Allow me to address these concerns one at a time.

Risk

There's no such thing as a completely risk-free investment, of any kind, but there are ways to reduce risk when purchasing real estate. When you buy in a good market with the five essential criteria, you're already taking some steps towards "insuring" your investment. In addition, buying a quality home located in a good neighborhood also reduces risk. A quality property needs fewer repairs than one in bad shape. In a good neighborhood, your tenants will be more likely to stay longer, pay on time, and take care of the property.

Checking Up

The last thing you want, of course, is for your house to become damaged or run down. It may seem that making an investment closer to home would provide some reassurance that things aren't going to hell in a handbasket.

Quality properties located in good markets and in good neighborhoods will get along without your constant vigilance very well—just as they would if they were located down the street from you. And even if your investment home is nearby, it's not as if you have the right to intrude on your tenants every few weeks and make a spot check of the premises. So, what are you going to do...drive by and gawk?

I can tell you right now, your house isn't going to look a lot different from month to month. Notwithstanding an Act of God (as insurance underwriters call earthquakes, tornadoes and hurricanes) houses don't change much and they tend to stay put.

Repairs and Maintenance

There is absolutely no law saying real estate investors need to be all-purpose handymen or women. I personally haven't picked up a hammer in years. For me, changing a light bulb is a major home improvement.

If you're like me, or even if you're a master carpenter who looks forward to the next remodeling project with unrestrained glee, do you really want to take on the burden of keeping your rental homes in tip-top shape?

No! You're busy!

So how do you take care of your investment home without spending your weekends painting, carpeting or fixing the plumbing?

You hire a property manager.

Even if your property is located near you, this is something I highly recommend. Property managers are pros. They know a lot more about taking care of your investment home than you do.

Traditionally, there's been a lot of resistance to this idea, but I've found this resistance is largely based on ignorance. We all hire professionals for different aspects of our lives—from attorneys and CPAs to housekeepers and pet-sitters. Hiring a property manager is no different: he or she provides us with expertise we don't have. Why is it acceptable to hire professionals for so many other purposes, but not to hire a professional to take care of our real estate investments? Strictly speaking, if you were involved in a lawsuit, could you go to the law library and research the law? Of course. But would you do it? Of course not. Similarly, could you manage your own house? Of course. But should you? Probably not.

Let a professional manage your property, even if it's close to where you live. This frees you up to live the life you want. Who really has the time or the desire to be a hands-on landlord? Not me! I own many homes spread across the country. If I didn't use property managers, I'd never have the time to run a business, write a book, or do anything else.

In fact, I'd probably be repairing a toilet at this very moment.

Vacancies

One of your biggest fears may be that your house is not going to rent. Buying a quality home in a good market minimizes this risk.

The vacancy problem I encounter most often is not an unrentable house...the owners are asking for too much rent. They haven't listened to the local experts, such as their realtor and property manager, and have insisted on listing the rental above what the market will bear—usually because they feel their house is, well, special.

It is much better to live with a little bit less cash flow than to price your rental so high it stands vacant. You don't have to "squeeze" the house for every nickel and dime to get something of great value back from your investment. Regarding cash flow, your tax benefits could improve that in the short or long term (depending on your income). It is inevitable that rental prices will increase with the cost of living and improve what the property brings in over time.

Still, you'll want to consider the vacancy rate for the market you've bought into. For some of the markets mentioned above, the average vacancy rate for quality single-family homes is 3%, meaning statistically, your house will be vacant for three months out of one hundred. If the rent is $1,400 per month, then you can deduct $42 from your cash flow figures. If you want to play it safe, deduct $70, or $100.

Just remember there's usually no such thing as an unrented house, there's only asking for too much rent.

Buy Where it Makes Sense to Buy

All I'm saying is, the best way to ensure your investment will be a good one is to buy where it makes sense to buy: in a good market, and in a good neighborhood. When I began investing, I bought lower-priced homes that weren't always so well located. Yes, they were "bargains." And you know what? If I'd started out buying quality homes in good neighborhoods, I would've made a lot more money by now (with fewer headaches). **I can't stress it strongly enough: buy quality homes in good neighborhoods.** It's one of the primary keys to making your investments work for you, and not the other way around.

Recently there is more and more evidence that brand new investors with little experience seek super-cheap homes in small towns with limited economies and job markets. One of my Silicon Valley investors recently sent me an article she read on LinkedIn. It looked professional and was decorated with beautiful graphs and charts. The core message though, was to buy super cheap homes in a very small town in Texas, far from any large metropolitan area. As of now, a decent home in any of the large metropolitan areas in Texas will easily cost $200,000 and above in good areas. That article talked about buying little homes in a little town for about $65,000! The writer talked about great cash flow, but his inexperience shone through. If the major (and possibly only) employer in that small town succumbs to Amazon or other economic forces and shuts down, where are the jobs? Who will rent? This is truly a disaster waiting to happen. Also buying homes for $65,000 quite likely means buying older, smaller homes in very iffy areas. All sure-fire recipes to create a bad investment. However, everyone can create a professional looking opinion piece these days, which in this case, caused even a powerful Silicon Valley-ite to do a double take. Luckily, a quick conversation with me uncovered the many faults in the inexperienced writer's thesis. Remember, looks can be deceiving—visually impressive does not automatically mean great content. Instead, use the simple criteria here to maximize the chances your investments work well.

Since a professional property manager is going to be looking after your property, why not buy where it makes sense to buy? Just because you happen to go to sleep at night in Los Angeles, does that mean all your investments have to be in Los Angeles? (The answer is, of course, no. If that wasn't your immediate response...consider reviewing this chapter again.)

 **REPLAY**

- ► You can't enjoy the benefits of real estate if you don't own real estate!
- ► Break the 30-minute "rule" and buy where it makes sense to buy.
- ► Keep in mind the five essential criteria: big city, good rental market where the numbers work, not a booming market, low median price, and in the Sun Belt States.
- ► It's much better to invest in a good market than to miss out altogether because you cannot invest in the "best" market.
- ► Don't let the "paralysis of over-analysis" stop you from investing.
- ► A deal doesn't have to be the deal of the century for it to work for you.
- ► Use professional property management to look after your properties.
- ► There's usually no such thing as an unrented house... there's only asking for too much rent.
- ► Buy quality homes in good neighborhoods.

CHAPTER 6

GETTING STARTED

Just as every journey begins with a single step, the road to your financial well-being begins with a single and attainable goal: buying your first investment home.

In a very real sense, buying your first investment home is the biggest hurdle. After all, you're traveling in uncharted territory...the new world of real estate investing. No doubt you'll have many questions (and even, perhaps, a few fears). But as you go through the process of buying that first investment home, your questions will be answered, and fears put to rest. I've found something else happens when you take this step: taking control of your financial future creates an increased confidence and sense of empowerment

In this chapter I'll encourage you to take stock of your finances and show what you should have in place before purchasing your first investment home. Whether you've already got money set aside or you need to raise money before you start, you'll find some handy tips for getting on the right track and staying there.

Becoming Financially Fit

Financial fitness is the basis of sound financial planning. By financially fit, I don't mean wealthy. What I mean is you have a solid understanding of your overall financial picture and a feasible budget that includes funds for investing. Becoming financially fit means knowing where you need to go and knowing how you'll get there.

Before you begin investing, it's a good idea to take a careful look at the big picture: what you own, what you owe, and how much cash and credit are available to you. To do this, you'll need to calculate your net worth and analyze your expenditures. Your annual income, the amount of debt you carry, your spending habits and your attitude about money will all play a part in the way you invest and how you structure your financial plan.

What is Net Worth?

Your net worth is the wealth you've accumulated to date: the amount left over after subtracting your liabilities from your assets. Assets include cash and savings, your home and personal property, stocks and bonds, real estate, privately owned businesses and retirement accounts. Liabilities include mortgage(s), car loans or lease, student or other loans, and credit card debt.

Your net worth is your financial barometer. It reveals the reserves you have to tap into—or the opposite, how your liabilities may be undermining your assets.

NET WORTH WORKSHEET

ASSETS

CASH AND SAVINGS	$

INVESTMENTS

STOCKS & MUTUAL FUNDS	
BONDS & BOND MUTUAL FUNDS	
STOCK OPTIONS	
VALUE OF PRIVATELY OWNED BUSINESS	
INVESTMENT REAL ESTATE	
CASH VALUE OF LIFE INSURANCE POLICIES	
OTHER INVESTMENTS	
TOTAL INVESTMENTS	$

RETIREMENT ACCOUNTS

IRAs	
401(k), 401(b)	
SELF-EMPLOYED PLANS (Keogh, etc.)	
ANNUITIES	
EST. VALUE OF COMPANY PENSION	
TOTAL RETIREMENT ACCOUNTS	$

HOME & PERSONAL PROPERTY

HOME	
VACATION HOME	
CARS, RECREATIONAL VEHICLES	
ART, COLLECTIBLES, JEWELRY, FURNISHINGS	
OTHER PERSONAL ASSETS	
TOTAL HOME & PERSONAL PROPERTY	$

TOTAL ASSETS

	$

LIABILITIES

MORTGAGE DEBT	
CAR LOANS/LEASE	
STUDENT LOANS	
CREDIT CARD BALANCES	
OTHER LOANS	
OTHER DEBT	
TOTAL LIABILITIES	$

NET WORTH (subtract liabilities from assets)

	$

Once you've calculated your net worth, you can easily see how your assets and liabilities stack up. While there's no hard-and-fast rule about how much you should have, or the percentage of liabilities to assets, you may discover some surprises. Perhaps your credit card debt has just about wiped out the positive figures in the assets section. Perhaps your home equity, stocks or retirement accounts have grown more than you anticipated. Your net worth statement shows how your assets and debts are distributed. When it comes time to raise cash or apply for a loan, this information will be very helpful to you.

PAUSE

It's important to update your net worth statement on a regular basis, typically once a year. It's a good way to keep in touch with your financial goals, and to make sure you're on the right path. Watching your net worth increase will help you stay focused and keep your enthusiasm high. Long-term investing requires discipline, and sometimes it can feel as if the rewards don't come soon enough. Your net worth statement transforms the abstract into black and white: you'll see the results of your hard work on the bottom line.

Insurance Coverage

An important part of financial fitness is making sure you and your assets are protected. Comprehensive insurance coverage is your primary defense against unforeseen—and potentially disastrous—events. It's true insurance premiums take a bite out of your budget and may seem, at times, like an unnecessary expense. Without proper insurance, however, you're gambling with your future, and with what you've already worked so hard to achieve.

There are four major areas of your life that need to be insured against loss: yourself, your dependents, your potential earnings, and your property.

Health Insurance

If you're fortunate, your employer has a group plan you can subscribe to, and your premiums may be included in your salary and benefits. Group plans generally offer the best coverage at the lowest price.

If you're self-employed, or if you can't get health insurance through your employer, you may want to contact a health insurance broker. (They are easy to find online.) Brokers will have access to a range of companies and can help you find a plan that fits your circumstances and budget. With the Affordable Care Act, it has become easier to purchase health insurance through the ACA health exchanges.

Life Insurance

Life insurance provides some peace of mind for those with dependents. Steer clear of "whole" or "universal" life insurance: the investment account associated with this kind of policy is usually low on returns and high on commissions. Go for term life insurance instead, basing your coverage amount on your income times the number of years you plan to keep working until retirement.

Disability Insurance

Your future income-earning ability is one of your biggest assets. If, because of illness or accident, you're unable to work, disability insurance will replace some or all of your lost income. Large companies often offer disability insurance to employees. If you're self-employed, you can find disability insurance through an insurance carrier or through a state- funded program. Check with insurance companies and your state disability insurance office to compare premiums and coverage.

Property Insurance

Homes, cars, and other property should be insured for their replacement cost. In addition, liability coverage protects you against lawsuits. Homeowners and auto insurance generally come with a certain amount of liability coverage; check your records to make sure yours is adequate.

You may also want to consider "umbrella" or excess liability insurance: a good rule of thumb is to insure yourself for at least twice the amount of your net worth.

Retirement Accounts

If you're eligible for an IRA plan, 401(k), their Roth varieties, 403(b), SEP, Keogh or any other tax-deferred retirement plan, take advantage of it. These plans offer tax shelters (which mean immediate benefits), and the power of compounding (which means long-term benefits). As with any account that grows through compounding—or interest earned on interest earned—the sooner you start, the more you stand to gain.

Using the investment options available to you is the surest way to become financially fit. Just because you've decided to invest in real estate doesn't mean you should ignore other viable investments. Basically, a retirement plan is a high-yield, favorably taxed, long-term savings account. Ideally, your financial strategy will include both a retirement account and real estate investments; the two are not mutually exclusive, but complementary.

How Much Money You'll Need to Get Started

Although many books and infomercials insist you can purchase real estate with "no money down," the truth is most real estate investments require an initial outlay of cash.

Exactly how much cash depends, of course, on the price of the property, the amount of leverage you use, and the closing costs. To keep it simple, though, I suggest that you set of goal of $40,000.

Sometimes It Feels Like a Lot...

Why $40,000? Because it's about enough to cover a 20% down payment and closing costs on $160,000 property, the low price of a quality single-family home in the markets I've recommended. (As of this writing, down payments of only 15% are possible, making the sum needed about $32,000. However, we will use $40,000 in our example.)

If you happen to have $40,000 laying around already—in a savings account, money market fund, or under the mattress— you can save yourself a little time and move right along to the next chapter.

But perhaps you don't have $40,000 laying around. Perhaps you're not sure how you're going to come up with $40,000, unless you plant a money tree in your backyard. If you're finding it difficult to sock away a couple hundred dollars into your savings account each month, a number with five figures can seem daunting.

...Sometimes It Doesn't

I know for a fact that raising $40,000 is possible for anyone. You may not be able to come up with that much money overnight, but if you keep your $40,000 goal firmly in mind, you will make it happen. Saving is just one way to raise money; there are many others, which I'll explain here. And yes, you can purchase real estate with less cash; I'll tell you more about that, too. If you're busy, however, the straightforward approach— putting 20% down—is often the best. It may mean some belt-tightening, but that's sometimes easier (and better for your financial fitness) than financing the entire amount.

It may help to remember this: $40,000 equals real property worth $160,000. In 20 years, the property may be worth over $250,000, by the most conservative measure (assuming the house doesn't appreciate more than the cost of living). At one and a half times the current inflation rate (which as you now know is, historically, the amount real estate appreciates each year), it will be worth over $306,000.

In other words: the $40,000 you sow today may reap over $300,000 in the future. To accumulate that much money without investing in real estate, you would have to save $15,000 every year for 20 years (actually a bit less due to interest you would accumulate on your savings, but with today's very low interest rates on savings, that is a minor effect).

If you have a hard time imagining what it will feel like to have $300,000 20 years from now, think about this: what if, 20 years ago, you'd invested $40,000 and had that $300,000 now?

If you're like most people, you'll wish you had invested $40,000 20 years ago. I can assure you that, 20 years from now, you're going to feel exactly the same way.

Does $40,000 still sound like a lot of money?

Reaching Your First Goal: $40,000

There are three primary ways to raise money: earn it, save it, or borrow it.

Of course, you can use any combination of the three. As you look over your net worth statement and budget, you'll discover the best way for you. I've listed the various ways to raise money in ascending order, from the most conservative (earning) to the most aggressive (borrowing). You'll need to be honest with yourself and look over your history. If you're currently trying to get out from under a load of credit card debt, the last thing you want to do is incur more. At the other end of the spectrum, if you're someone who never pays a cent in interest, you may find you can benefit from using the credit available to you.

Eight Ways to Raise Money

Earning It

Selling Unused Assets

Saving It

Borrowing It

- From Friends or Relatives

- Equity Loan

- Against 401(k)

- From a Bank

- From Credit Cards (Beware!!!)

Earning It

If your job and family have you constantly on the go, taking on part-time employment to earn more money is probably out of the question.

But there may be things you haven't thought of, such as home sales, or a sideline hobby or craft. Or perhaps you can use your special expertise to work as a part-time consultant in your field.

If you have few assets, and a low income that's already stretched to the limit, a part-time business may be your answer. Benefits include flexibility—you can set your own hours—and tax deductions against your income, which may lead to tax savings. (You'll need to peruse Schedule C, Profit or Loss from Business, of the IRS' 1040 Form to see how this may apply to your particular situation, or ask a tax professional.)

Selling Unused Assets

A corollary to earning more income is raising money by selling items you no longer want or need. No, I don't mean a yard sale...but what about that boat or RV that's been gathering dust in the driveway? The timeshare you never have time to use? The empty plot of land in Northern Idaho Uncle Willie left to you? The piano no one plays?

Take a good look at the things you own. If they're not appreciating assets, and they don't have sentimental value (such as family heirlooms), you might want to consider selling them. After all, we're talking about your future. Why let your money sit around in unused assets when it can be working for you?

Saving It

You may wonder why it's hard to save regardless of how much money you make. You're not alone. On average, people are saving only 5% of their after-tax income.

Learning to budget and allocate funds for your future is essential to becoming financially fit. In fact, the money you set aside for investments is the most important part of your budget. Unfortunately, too many people see it as the least important, something they do only if there's enough left over...and all too often, there's nothing left over.

To make a profound difference in your future, you must reorganize your priorities, and place investment funds right up there with food, shelter and insurance. To do this, you'll need to look at how you've spent money in the past. Collect all your receipts from the last three months (if you're self-employed, or have a fluctuating income, you may want to go back six months), and fill out this form:

EXPENDITURES WORKSHEET

Mortgage or Rent _____
Property Tax _____
Homeowners/Renters Insurance _____
Utilities _____
Furnishings, Maintenance _____
Phone and Internet _____
Other Household Expenses _____

Groceries _____
Dining Out _____

Car Loan/Lease _____
Fuel, Maintenance & Repairs _____
Auto Insurance _____
Other Transportation (taxi, bus, etc.) _____

Federal, State, Local Taxes _____
Social Security/Pension Contributions _____
Tax on Investment Income _____

Retirement Plan Contributions _____
Passbook/Money Market Savings _____

Health Insurance _____
Medical Services, Drugs not covered by insurance _____
Health Club Dues _____

Child Care _____

Movies, Theater, Cable TV _____
Books, Magazines, Videos _____

Apparel, Shoes _____
Personal Care (haircuts, massage) _____
Laundry, Dry Cleaning _____

Vacations, Travel _____

Miscellaneous Expenses _____

TOTAL MONTHLY EXPENSES $_____

Evaluating your spending habits is probably the most painful part of the process, but it's also one of the most enlightening. Most people are shocked when they see just how much they spend each month on things nonessentials. If you and your spouse both work, it's probably even more of a shock. The busier you are, the more money you're likely to spend (and the less time you must track exactly how you're spending it).

There's only one way to save without earning more money: spend less. Looking over your expenditures, you're sure to find areas you can economize. In fact, your spending habits are the first place to look for cash.

It may be time to bite the bullet and trade off some of the luxuries you enjoy now—frequent dining out, or expensive vacations—in order to begin building your future. But don't forget to look at the little luxuries you take for granted. If you can save just $20 a day—the price of a deli lunch and a café latte—you'll save $7300 a year. If you and your spouse save $20 a day each, that's $14,600—or one investment home every three years or so!

Just Say "No" to Consumer Spending

We grew up in an age of instant credit and immediate gratification. It's hard to resist the appeal of buying now and paying later, and it can be a difficult habit to break. But it's a main reason people find it hard to save and to plan for the future.

Overuse of credit for things like cars, electronics, vacations, and other lifestyle goodies is a big trap that's all too easy to fall into. Add up your credit card balances and car loans to see what you're paying in interest each year.

The money you throw away on interest isn't the only price you pay for buying now and paying later. If the new car, widescreen TV, and hot tub mean you don't have anything left to save or invest each month, you're robbing yourself of a prosperous future.

For example, let's assume in 2020, the average cost of a new car is about $37,850 per Kelley Blue Book. Even with a low interest rate (say 2%), the payments on a five year loan with no down payment will be approximately $663 a month: that's $7,956 each year for five years, or $39,780. In 20 years, what will you have to show for this expense? A 20-year-old car. If, instead, you'd invested that $39,780 in real estate (buying a nice home for about $160,000), you'd likely own property worth over $300,000.

Then, you can buy any car you want...in a few different colors even.

The real, bottom line secret to financial planning is learning to delay gratification, to live with a little less now so you'll have more—much more—in the future. It's not complicated, and it doesn't require any special know-how, just some discipline and determination.

Creating Your New, Financially Fit Budget

Once you're recovered from the shock of your monthly expenditures, it's time to make a plan to get your spending under control. On the next page is a budget worksheet for you to complete. Notice that "investment funds" is listed right up top, along with your mortgage, insurance premiums, and retirement accounts.

BUDGET WORKSHEET

Investment Funds _____

Retirement Plan Contributions _____

Passbook/Money Market Savings _____

Life Insurance _____

Disability Insurance _____

Mortgage or Rent _____

Property Tax _____

Homeowners/Renters Insurance _____

Utilities _____

Furnishings, Maintenance _____

Phone and Internet _____

Other Household Expenses _____

Groceries _____

Dining Out _____

Car Loan/Lease _____

Fuel, Maintenance & Repairs _____

Auto Insurance _____

Other Transportation (taxi, bus, etc.) _____

Federal, State, Local Taxes _____

Social Security or Pension Contributions _____

Tax on Investment Income _____

Health Insurance _____

Medical Services, Drugs not covered by insurance _____

Health Club Dues _____

Child Care _____

Movies, Theater, Cable TV _____

Books, Magazines, Videos _____

Apparel, Shoes _____

Personal Care (haircuts, massage) _____

Laundry, Dry Cleaning _____

Vacations, Travel _____

TOTAL MONTHLY BUDGET $ _____

Create a budget that reprioritizes your expenses, and places money for investment before other expenses (such as clothing, dining out, entertainment, and other areas you may be able to cut back on).

Set Up a Separate Account

Opening a separate account for your investment funds is an excellent way to keep your budget on track and your goal firmly in sight. Whether you're saving to buy your first investment home or to finance further investments, decide on a set amount you can deposit each month, and stick to it.

If you're on an accelerated savings plan, or already have some cash set aside, a regular savings account will do. However, a money market fund (available from mutual fund companies), combines the convenience of a savings or checking account with a higher yield (or return) on your money.

When you contribute to a money market fund, you're buying shares in a large portfolio of money market securities such as Treasury bills, commercial paper, and other cash equivalents. As with a savings account, your money is safe (the principal is not at risk), and liquid (you can make deposits and withdrawals just as you can with a savings or checking account), but a money market fund will grow at a faster rate than a savings account.

Another Way to Save

If you have a hard time sticking to a budget, there may be a way to save that will work for you: enlist the government's help. If you tend to spend all your income every month, reduce the number of tax exemptions on your W-2 form. More tax dollars will be taken out of each paycheck, which you'll get back, months later, in the form of a tax refund.

This isn't the best way to save, because the feds, and not you, earn interest on the money deducted from your earnings. Of course, when you get your refund, it must go straight into your money market fund or savings account. And in the meantime, put away those credit cards!

If, on the other hand, you receive a large refund each year, you may want to increase the number of exemptions. With more exemptions, fewer tax dollars will be taken out of your paycheck, and you can put the extra into your money market fund. This way, you can watch your investment account grow each month, and earn dividends while you're saving.

Borrowing It

If you don't have cash on hand, and you'd like to start investing right away, borrowing may be the answer. The sooner you begin investing, the sooner you'll see benefits, so I always recommend acting as quickly as possible (with a few caveats).

If you've got friends or relatives with deep pockets, they may be willing to finance a down payment. If you have equity in your home, 401(k), or other retirement account, you may be able to borrow against your own assets. If you have good credit and a steady income, you may be able to borrow from a bank.

There are pros and cons to each of these methods. But before you contemplate taking on more debt, look at the debt you already have. What are your monthly payments? Will you be able to take on an additional monthly payment, and still adhere to your new, financially fit budget? If you have credit card debt, are you just paying the minimum every month, or are you able to pay them off in full?

If you're already carrying a lot of debt—especially credit card debt—you should consider consolidating or paying off those debts before taking on more.

Borrowing from Friends or Relatives

Hitting up a rich friend or relative may be a fast and easy way to raise the cash you need to get started. If your parents are financially secure, they may be more than willing to offer you a loan, especially after you've shown them it will be used to finance a serious, sound, long-term investment.

Before you begin calling up everyone you know, consider how borrowing money from friends or relatives might affect your relationship. Think about what may happen if, for some reason, you're unable to pay it back. And what if your benefactor suddenly goes broke and needs the money returned right away?

If everything goes exactly as planned, borrowing from a friend or relative can give you a head start. Chances are they'll offer favorable rates, or even a tax-free gift of up to $15,000 (as of 2020). But the unforeseen does sometimes happen, and if you want to maintain good relationships, you need to make sure all involved parties have a complete understanding of the terms of the loan.

Put everything in writing: the loan amount, interest rate, and payment schedule. Discuss all possibilities that may arise, and how you'll deal with them. And put that in writing, too.

Borrowing from Home Equity

Equity is the difference between your home's current market value and the amount you owe. Your net worth statement should show you how much equity you have in your home.

Assuming you can afford the monthly payments of a second mortgage, and your current debt load is not too great, an equity loan is perhaps the easiest and most cost-effective way to borrow money from yourself.

Many lenders offer equity loans. Because the loan is secured against your property, interest rates for equity loans are generally lower than rates for unsecured loans.

Interest deductions on home equity lines have changed with the 2018 tax law. Please check with your accountant to see what is deductible and what is no longer deductible.

Borrowing from Retirement Plans

Some retirement plans allow you to borrow money against your retirement account to buy a home; your ability to do this is dependent on the plan managers who set it up.

The advantage of borrowing against your retirement account to raise a down payment is you actually pay back your own account, with interest, rather than paying interest to a mortgage company. The disadvantage is, if you don't pay the loan back in a specified amount of time, it is considered a distribution. If you're under 59 ½ years of age you'll have to pay a penalty plus income taxes on the amount you borrowed. (Very bad!)

Borrowing from a Bank

In these times of mergers and consolidations, when local banks are swallowed up by national corporations, it's harder than ever to qualify for a bank loan. Even if the local branch manager is your tennis buddy, chances are your loan application will be sent to a loan service center in another state. It will be processed by a computer that cares about only three things: your social security number, your annual income and your credit rating.

If you have a high annual income and good credit rating, the computer might spit out a favorable answer. Otherwise, you're just plain out of luck. Computers don't care about extenuating factors, such as your trustworthiness, your willingness to give up vacations for the next five years, or that your grandmother is rich, and you'll inherit her fortune (of course, if that's true, you may not need the bank after all). Typically, the bank manager can't override the decision of the ultimate number-cruncher.

It may seem that the old adage is true now more than ever: banks only lend money to those who don't need it.

Is there a way to get around this? Yes and no. If it means playing a kind of round-robin game by opening as many credit lines in as many banks as possible, then no. File that idea under hare-brained schemes (and that may be an injustice to rabbit intelligence). Unless you're a financial wizard, playing games with banks and multiple lines of credit is a sure way to mess up your credit rating.

In case you haven't noticed it, banks are not very playful. It's better to approach them as you would an unfriendly giant you hope to recruit as a player for your basketball team. You've got to woo him a little, and offer him his favorite food—in this case, your money.

Having a relationship with your bank is the best way to establish yourself as a worthy loan applicant. By relationship, I don't mean dinners and flowers, but keeping all your accounts in the same place, and getting to know the bank manager and loan officers. If you feel like small potatoes at your current bank, look for a smaller, more local operation that may be more appreciative of your business—this could include a community bank or credit union. Every time you need a loan, be it a home equity, car or business loan, look to your bank for financing. After paying a few secured loans back on time, they'll get to know you as a safe credit risk. In the world of banking relationships, that's as good as being engaged.

Borrowing from Credit Cards (Beware!!!)

Borrowing money from credit cards is an option, but not one I recommend. Credit card money is probably the most expensive money you can borrow. Credit cards charge high interest, and the interest you pay is not tax deductible.

Before you take cash advances from your credit cards, consider other ways you can borrow. Any one of the other possibilities outlined above is better for your financial fitness.

If borrowing from credit cards is the only way for you to raise a down payment for your first investment home, be certain you meet the following criteria:

- You have excellent credit, and you plan to keep it that way.
- You have very little outstanding debt.
- You can afford the extra payments.
- You're responsible. Very responsible.

In other words, you have enough income, and enough discipline, to pay off the amount drawn from your credit cards within a few months. If you allow the credit card balances to remain much longer than that, you're going to pay a very steep price. Above all, be aware of the cost involved before you borrow.

What "No Money Down" Really Means

"No money down" simply means the property is 100% leveraged. In other words, the purchaser has borrowed the entire amount, including the down payment, to buy the property.

In the "no money down" method that gained popularity in the 1980s and 1990s, financing is offered by the seller. This was partly, especially in the 1980s, due to the very high mortgage interest rates, which made many buyers reluctant to get bank loans. Seller financing is not nearly as widespread these days. Just because it's possible doesn't make it probable. The overwhelming majority of people who sell their homes need to cash out.

Another thing rarely mentioned is the type of property offered by sellers who are willing to finance. Quality single-family homes in good markets rarely, if ever, have motivated sellers. Unfortunately, the "gurus" of the past have made buying with no money down more important than buying quality real estate. In the final analysis, how you finance the property isn't as important as buying real estate that will be a sound, long-term investment (i.e. quality homes in good neighborhoods). Even if it's 100% financed, a bad property is still a bad property!

Five "No Money Down" Techniques

The types of borrowing I've mentioned above are "no money down" techniques. When you borrow the down payment from:

- a friend or family member,
- your own home equity,
- a retirement account,
- a bank,
- or credit cards,

that's also 100% leverage, or no money down.

If 100% leverage works for you, do it. Remember, however, it will mean higher monthly payments and you may have to live with negative cash flow for a while (depending on what the interest rates are). However, this may lower your tax liability, which could mitigate the negative cash flow somewhat. If your budget can handle it, and it's the only way for you to begin investing, then you may want to consider it.

REPLAY

- ▸ Buying one investment home should be your first goal.
- ▸ Becoming financially fit means understanding your overall financial picture and setting goals.
- ▸ Comprehensive insurance coverage is your primary defense against unforeseen events.
- ▸ Contribute to at least one retirement plan.
- ▸ The $40,000 you sow today could reap over $300,000 in 20 years.
- ▸ Learning to budget and allocate funds for investing is essential to your financial fitness.
- ▸ Just say "no" to consumer spending.
- ▸ Set up a separate account for investment funds. Know the cost of borrowing before you borrow.
- ▸ No Money Down simply means 100% financing.

CHAPTER 7

FINANCING

Even if you're able to pay cash for an investment property, it isn't in your best interest to do so. Financing the property often means using leverage (long-term fixed-rate loans) and gaining tax benefits: the duo that makes your money and net worth grow.

In this chapter, I'll explain the loan types you should choose from, what lenders look for in a borrower, the importance of good credit, and the documents you'll need to complete your loan application.

Selecting a Mortgage

Financing is all too often a stressful and confusing part of purchasing your investment home. There are so many mortgage lenders, offering an ever-increasing number of loan options, it can be difficult to know where to begin. Throw in financing jargon—points, prepaids, APR, PMI, caps—and you might wish you never started.

Happily, you don't need to be a financial wizard or a mortgage maven to secure favorable financing for your investment property.

Financing doesn't have to be complicated. Even though many loan types are available, there are only three types I recommend. Any one of these common loan types will provide you with long-term, safe, secure financing with no unpleasant surprises.

Fixed-Rate Mortgages

When you get a fixed-rate mortgage, you know exactly what your monthly payments will be. No matter what the term of the loan, your payments will not change.

A 30-year loan offers the most flexibility. Since the payments are lower than a 15-year loan, it frees up more of your income for other purposes, such as funding retirement accounts or other investments. Or you can make extra payments on the principal and pay off the loan sooner. In fact, the 30-year loan contains the 15-year loan, or the 18-year loan, or the 10-year loan: you can pay it off in the number of years that fits your financial plan.

Fixed-rate loans generally carry a slightly higher interest rate than adjustable or short-term loans, because the lender is making a commitment to lend money at a fixed-rate over a long term. Remember, however, that inflation will effectively reduce the amount of your mortgage payment year after year. A fixed-rate loan with a static payment over the life of your investment is the equivalent of a monthly payment that will erode over time.

It probably goes without saying that you'll want the lowest interest rate possible, although there are a few other things to consider when selecting a loan (see "Shopping for a Loan" later in this chapter). But not everyone will qualify for the lowest interest rate available; the rate you're offered will depend upon your creditworthiness and other factors. If the interest rate for fixed-rate loans is high (well above today's investors' rate of about 3.5% or so), or if the only fixed-rate loan you can qualify for is two or three points above the best rate, you may want to consider two other financing options: an adjustable rate mortgage or a hybrid mortgage.

Adjustable-Rate Mortgages

Adjustable-rate mortgages (ARMs) have a variable interest rate that rises or falls according to the index to which they are tied. Most ARMs adjust annually, but some adjust monthly, or every six months.

The first-year rate (or "teaser" rate) of an ARM is usually a point or two below the interest rate for fixed-rate loans. The interest rate on many, but not all, ARMs is capped, meaning it can rise only a certain number of percentage points (usually five) over the life of the loan. For instance, if your starting interest rate is 2.5%, and you have a five-point cap, the highest interest rate possible on your ARM is 7.5%.

The rise of the interest rate on an ARM is limited to either one or two percentage points each year, so the interest rate can't rise from 2.5% to 7.5% overnight but would take several years to rise to its highest rate. An ARM can also go down, if the index to which it is tied goes down.

ARMS can be beneficial when rates on fixed-rate loans are high (currently it would be, say, at least well above 4.5%), or if you can't qualify for a low interest fixed-rate loan. Because you usually know when and how much your ARM is going to rise, you can begin with an ARM, then refinance a few years later, when the interest rate on a fixed-rate loan is lower than your ARM. By then, you'll have equity in the property, and it may be easier for you to qualify for a lower interest fixed-rate loan.

Hybrid Loans

As the name implies, hybrid loans are a combination of fixed-rate and adjustable loans. Hybrid loans (also called intermediate ARMs) start out like a fixed-rate loan, with a fixed interest rate for a term of three, five, or seven years (they're generally referred to, respectively, as a 3/1, 5/1 and 7/1; a pure ARM is often referred to as a 1/1). After the initial term, the loan converts to an ARM, adjusting every six to 12 months.

The starting interest rate of a hybrid loan, like an ARM, is lower than a fixed-rate loan, but because it's locked in for a longer time than the six-month or one-year teaser rate of an ARM, it's higher than an adjustable.

During times when fixed-rate loans have low interest rates, the difference between ARMs, hybrids and fixed-rate loans can be as little as one or one-half of one percent. During these periods, fixed-rate loans offer the best long-term value. When interest rates rise, and the difference between fixed-rate and adjustable rate loans is greater, then ARMs and hybrids can offer considerable savings—at least for the first few years.

Take on an adjustable or hybrid loan only if you can't qualify for a 30-year, fixed-rate loan or when interest rates for fixed-rates loans are high. If you do this, however, refinance to a 30-year, fixed-rate loan when interest rates decline and it's possible to lock-in a low rate. Refinancing does have some costs involved, but they are usually recouped over time when you refinance to a lower rate. Also, in many cases the refinancing costs can be included in the new loan balance so you don't have to pay cash for them, but instead borrow them at a low rate over 30 years.

 **PAUSE**

Why I Recommend 30-year, Fixed-Rate Loans

As an investor, your safest course is to go with a fixed-rate loan. This keeps your payments stable over the life of your investment, which helps you estimate cash flow, expenses, profits, taxes, and so on. But my main reason for recommending it is the cost of a 30-year fixed-rate erodes as the cost of living rises. Don't fear the 30-year term. You can pay the loan off at any time—after 5, 11 or 16 years. usually without paying a penalty. Thirty-year, fixed-rate financing is the ultimate no-brainer. Once you have it in place, you don't have to think about it again.

Shopping for a Loan: Comparing Costs

The cost of a mortgage involves more than just interest rates. The loan package, or "product," as it's known in the industry, consists of an interest rate, points, and loan-related fees. Points are always paid at settlement, or "closing," as it's generally called. So are many of the fees, hence the term "closing costs."

The annual percentage rate, or APR, is the combination of the loan's interest rate, points and fees, and indicates the "true" cost of the loan. If all lenders used the same method to calculate APRs, selecting the lowest-priced loan would be easy. Unfortunately, they don't. The only way to know the actual cost of a loan is to know the price of the fees associated with that loan.

At the beginning of the mortgage process, the lender is required to provide the borrower a Loan Estimate that outlines a good faith estimate of key mortgage terms such as interest rate and closing costs within three business days of the borrower submitting a mortgage application. At the end of the mortgage process, the lender is required to provide the borrower a Closing Disclosure that outlines the final, actual terms of the mortgage at least three business days before the mortgage closes.

Points and Fees

A point is an up-front fee paid to the lender at closing. One point equals 1% of the loan amount. For example, one point of a $150,000 mortgage would be $1,500, two points would be $3,000, and so on.

There are two kinds of points. Origination points are for processing the loan (typically, one point, or one percent of the loan amount, is charged for this service).

Discount points are paid by the borrower to reduce the interest rate of the loan. It's common to be offered a choice of loans with various combinations of interest rates and points; the more points, the lower the rate, and vice versa. As the borrower, you can decide whether you're better off paying a higher interest rate or "buying down" the rate by paying points at closing.

Loan fees fall into one of two groups. The first includes amounts paid to state and local governments, including city, county and state recording fees, and prepaid property taxes. The second includes the costs of getting a mortgage, with fees for title insurance, appraisals, credit checks, loan origination and documentation fees, commitment and processing fees, hazard and mortgage insurance, title insurance and interest prepayments.

The payments to state and local governments should be the same with every lender. The fees in the second group, however, can vary from lender to lender, and are a substantial part of your loan cost.

Because closing practices vary from region to region, it's difficult to provide accurate estimates for these costs. Typically, they range from 2.5% to 5% of the loan amount. You can shop around for competitive pricing, and in some instances, you can negotiate lower fees. Especially negotiable items include document preparation fees and lender's attorney fees.

Don't forget: points and interest rates may also be negotiable. The mortgage industry is very competitive, and a lender won't deny a loan to an approved borrower just because you asked for a 25% discount on the points (they might say no to your request, but they won't refuse the loan). You won't know if it's possible to get a better deal unless you ask!

Private Mortgage Insurance:
To Pay or Not to Pay?

When you make a down payment of less than 20%, lenders require you to carry private mortgage insurance, or PMI. Common (mortgage industry) wisdom holds that borrowers with less than a 20% stake in their property are more likely to default. Private mortgage insurance protects lenders (not borrowers) from financial loss when a homeowner goes into foreclosure.

Typically, a portion of the PMI premium is paid at closing, and a monthly payment representing 1/12 of the annual premium is paid along with the principal and interest of the loan.

The cost of PMI for investment properties is higher than for owner-occupied properties and, for this reason, some investors prefer to use a 20% down payment instead of 15% and avoid PMI altogether. (Especially since the interest rate is also somewhat higher on a loan obtained with 15% down vs 20%.) On the flip side, I've often financed investment properties with 15% down, paid PMI, and still had a positive monthly cash flow.

Personally, I prefer to use as much leverage as possible; that additional 5% down payment could be used towards the purchase of another investment property. Remember, PMI is not permanent. Depending on the loan, it drops off in the future once you have exceeded a certain equity threshold in the property, usually within a few years.

Generally, when you compare the price of PMI to an extra 5% cash out of your pocket, the PMI wins. However, if you're older, have a lot of cash, and need immediate cash flow, use a 20% or even 30% down payment and skip the PMI.

Where Do Mortgages Come From?

So, where do you go to get a loan? These days, finding a lender isn't hard; in fact, there's a bewildering number out there. If you already own a home, you're probably inundated with daily offers for equity, home improvement, and debt consolidation loans.

Lenders can be grouped into two categories: 1) commercial banks, credit unions, and savings and loan associations; and 2) mortgage banks.

Commercial banks, credit unions and savings and loan associations are the first places most people think of when contemplating mortgages, but they don't always offer the most favorable rates. If you're a member of a credit union or have sizeable accounts at a bank or savings and loan, however, it may be worthwhile to inquire about their loan products and pricing (remember, relationships count).

Mortgage banks are companies that originate, close and service mortgage loans. Unlike the financial institutions mentioned above, they don't offer traditional bank services. Since they focus solely on making mortgage loans, they generally offer attractive programs and rates.

A very important consideration is to make sure the lender can actually close loans successfully and in a timely manner in the state you are buying your investment in. Lenders have to be licensed in the state in which you are interested. In addition, some lenders may not have a smooth and efficient process in the state you are buying in, which can cause delays and even late fees charged by the seller, and potentially even a contract termination due to poor performance by the lender. I recommend asking the local broker in the market in which you are buying to recommend a lender they know can close loans well in their market.

FNMA Limits on Number of Loans

Federal National Mortgage Association (FNMA and referred to as Fannie Mae) sets the rules for buying loans on the secondary markets, and as of 2020, it limits the number of mortgages an individual can have to a total of 10. That includes loans on your primary and secondary residence. This 10-loan limit applies to everyone, whether it's a street cleaner or Warren Buffet.

If you are married, and each spouse earns and can qualify for a loan separately, then the limit is 10 per spouse for a total of 20. While it is usually a "knee jerk reaction" to get loans in both spouses' names, it is wise to get a loan only in one of their names, to preserve the higher limit, should that couple wish to extend their investment program beyond 10 properties. FNMA even allows one spouse to qualify by themselves, but the property can be owned in both spouses' names. Check with your lender.

Mortgage Brokers

Mortgage brokers are intermediaries between borrowers and lenders. Typically, they have access to a wide variety of lenders, including commercial banks and mortgage banks, and can offer you a choice of loans. Brokers can help you complete your loan application and can explain any differences between the loans offered to you. If you're turned down by a lender, they can quickly place your application with another one and speed up the approval process.

Although most brokers charge a fee for their service (some are paid a commission by the lender), they can save you money by shopping your loan application to various lenders. They can also save you a great deal of time. They're in the middle of the mortgage market every day and will (or should) know a competitively-priced loan when they see it. They know how to talk to lenders and will be able to explain the sometimes mystifying jargon of all those loan documents you've got to sign.

Another advantage of working with a broker is you won't have to create a new loan application package every time you apply to a lender.

They'll have your loan application and supporting documents on file, ready to go the next time you apply for a loan with, perhaps, just a little updating.

For all these reasons it may be worthwhile finding a trustworthy, dedicated broker with whom you can establish a long-term working relationship. Tell them you're planning to create a portfolio of investment homes; if you have a timetable in mind (i.e. two years, five years, 10 years), let them know it. They'll be able to keep you abreast of changes in the loan market and they'll appreciate the repeat business.

How do you find a mortgage broker? We (our company) can recommend someone we might be using at the time, or the local broker in the market you are investing in might recommend one to you. Or you can ask your friends if they have worked (and had good results) with a broker in your area. As always, personal endorsements are a good place to start.

If you can't locate a broker through word-of-mouth, contact your local branch of the Mortgage Brokers Association for referrals.

Since we are talking about buying in various markets in different states, sometimes it is more convenient to work with a big bank, which may have a group dedicated to investor loans in all 50 states. That could be superior to a loan broker who may only be licensed in a limited number of states. We can also recommend such a group to you as the need arises. One of the things I value is performance: has this bank closed many loans in different markets in a timely manner? Are they capable? Experience tends to show these attributes, and we will be happy to connect you.

What Lenders Look For

When you apply for a loan, lenders evaluate what they call the "Four Cs": collateral, cash, capacity and credit.

Collateral refers to the property itself, which in the U.S. is usually the sole collateral for the loan. An appraisal will be made to confirm the property's value will support the amount of the loan.

Cash refers to the down payment. Lenders typically require a down payment of 15 to 20% (or more) of the property's sale price, along with closing costs.

Capacity refers to your income, debt, and cash reserves. Lenders will look at check stubs or tax returns, credit reports and bank statements to determine your ability to repay the loan.

Credit refers to your credit history: how you've handled your debts in the past. Your credit report will reveal the amounts and terms of past and present loans, how you've repaid them (currently and in the past).

The Importance of Good Credit

The very first thing lenders do after receiving your application is obtain a copy of your credit report. You can get a copy from them (after all, you're usually paying for it; the lender will typically tack on $25 to as much as $75 for this service, and some lenders don't charge at all). But it's advisable to check out your credit report before you approach a lender. If there's an error or any negative information, you can rectify it—or explain it—before you apply for a loan.

The Fair Credit Reporting Act authorizes you to obtain a copy of your credit report from any credit reporting agency for a reasonable charge. If you have been denied credit, disclosure is free within 30 days from the agency that provided your data to the lender. Generally, the letter informing you credit was declined will list the reporting agency and provide an address to send your request. There is also the ability to get a completely free credit report once a year at freecreditreport.com.

 **PAUSE**

CREDIT REPORTING SERVICES

Knowing your credit score and monitoring your credit regularly is important. You may want to consider using a service that provides information from all three credit reporting bureaus: Equifax, Experian and TransUnion. Various services offer monitoring of your credit reports from all three bureaus for a fee. These change from time to time, so shop around on the web to get the package that suits your needs.

However, it's a good idea to keep abreast of any changes to your credit report and monitor it regularly. As an investor, keeping your credit in good standing is very important: it can be the difference between getting a loan or being denied, and will affect the interest rate and down payment of any loan you're offered. Those with higher credit ratings will be offered lower rates and more favorable loans. Your credit report plays an important part in your success with lenders.

What's on Your Credit Report?

Your credit report will list:

- Your name, date of birth, and Social Security Number;
- Your present and former addresses;
- Present and former employment;
- Public records on file: judgements, tax liens, and bankruptcies;
- Account information: mortgage(s) car loan(s), student or other loans (with payment histories) outstanding balances and credit limits;
- Late payments, delinquent payments, foreclosures etc.
- List of companies that have requested your credit report in the past six months.

Mistakes do occur and most often they're not in your favor. As you review your credit report, you should carefully check these items:

- Is your name, address, date of birth and Social Security Number correct?
- Do all the accounts listed belong to you?
- Are all the accounts listed accurately?
- Has all negative information been deleted after seven years? (Chapter 7 bankruptcy is removed after 10 years, foreclosures after 7 years.)
- Do you recognize all listed inquiries?

Correcting Errors and Bad Credit

If you discover inaccurate information on your credit report, you must write to the credit bureau responsible, and explain why the information is not correct. Under the Fair Credit Reporting Act, the credit bureau must investigate the matter, and correct any information it finds is not reported accurately. Information that cannot be verified should be deleted.

If you disagree with the results of the credit bureau's investigation, you are entitled to write a brief dispute statement that, at your request, will be included in future credit reports. If the negative information on your credit report is true, make sure it is removed as soon as legally possible. In the meantime, do your utmost to improve your rating by paying your bills on time.

The Loan Application Checklist

Whether you're working on your own or with a broker, you'll need to collect many documents required for your loan application.

Income: W-2 forms or recent pay stubs. If you're self- employed, you may need to show tax returns for the previous two years.

Assets: Checking and savings account statements for the previous two to three months, real estate owned, automobile titles, list of savings bonds, stocks or other investments and their current market value.

Debts: Most recent mortgage statement; copies of alimony or child support payments. (Most information about your credit card debt, car loans or other loans will be gleaned from the lender's copy of your credit report, although they may ask you to provide additional documents such as credit card bills for the previous few months.)

Information About the Property: Copy of the purchase contract, cancelled deposit check.

Each lender has its own documentation requirements. To save time, call ahead and ask which supporting documents are necessary to complete the loan application.

Create a Loan Application File

Once you've rifled your desk drawers, file cabinets and shoe boxes for all the documents listed above, make copies of everything and create a separate file folder so they'll be handy the next time you apply for a loan.

You may also want to add credit report updates, correspondence regarding errors on your credit reports, confirmation letters for the closing of a credit card account or personal loan, and documents regarding changes in marital status.

If you have all the supporting materials for your loan application at hand, you'll find that the process of getting a loan is much less stressful.

REPLAY

- ► When interest rates are low, 30-year fixed-rate loans are an investor's best choice.

- ► Consider an ARM or hybrid mortgage when interest rates are high.

- ► The true cost of a loan, or APR, includes the interest rate, points and fees. Compare the Loan Estimates from the lenders.

- ► Leveraging your investment with a 15% down payment and PMI means less cash out-of-pocket, but 20% with no PMI may be preferable.

- ► Mortgage brokers have access to hundreds of lenders

- ► Groups inside large banks can lend to investors in all 50 states.

- ► Obtain a copy of your credit report and correct errors or bad credit before you shop for a loan.

CHAPTER 8

SELECTING A PROPERTY

When you follow the "Remote Control" method, selecting an investment property is relatively easy. Reasonably priced, newer, high quality investment homes in good neighborhoods are available in many cities in the U.S. (as outlined in Chapter 5). Over the years, we have found that establishing relationships with our local brokers in the various marketplaces, and working with them to purchase hundreds or thousands of properties for ICG investors, creates a good base whereby we can look at the properties selected by the local brokers and know they are very likely to be worth investing in.

However, there are some key features you should keep in mind as you look for the right single-family home. In this chapter, I'll cover the elements you should be thinking about as you and your realtor search for an investment property, along with tips on negotiating the purchase price, preparing a cash flow analysis, and an overview of what happens during escrow and closing.

Location, Location, Location

I've said it before, and I'll say it again: buy where it makes sense to buy. You want a high-quality property that will keep appreciating over a long term, which means buying only in markets with the five essential criteria (listed again so you do not need to revisit Chapter 5):

- **Big City**
- **Good Rental Market Where the Numbers Work**
- **Not a Booming Market**
- **Low Median Price**
- **Sun Belt**

More Detail on Good Neighborhoods

A good location is, by definition, a good neighborhood. Good neighborhoods, like good markets, also have essential features. The first recognizable feature of a good neighborhood is that it's composed of primarily single-family homes: there should be very few or no duplexes, fourplexes, apartment buildings, or condominiums.

This may seem a bit stringent, but time and experience have shown me that buying single-family homes in neighborhoods composed primarily of single-family homes is a much safer, sounder investment than buying homes in "mixed" neighborhoods. It promises the greatest rewards and the least trouble over the long-term. (Note: there are exceptions to any rule, and having duplexes, triplexes or even fourplexes that are located in a quality area could still be okay investments.)

Good neighborhoods also have good schools. Be aware that you should not be hung up on excellent schools or very highly-rated schools, necessarily. It's what fits that local market, and what the norm is. Try not to bring the norms from where you live into the market where you are buying. Talk to your local broker. They're the places in the city where most families want to live. They're safe, clean, and often have a homeowner's association that provides guidelines to help ensure rising home values.

In good neighborhoods, most homes are owned by the people who live in them. "Pride of ownership" keeps the neighborhood's property values high, and makes it a more stable, safe, and desirable place to live. This ensures the value of your rental property and keeps its value and rental rate rising over the years. Even when I purchase numerous homes in the same area, I make sure I don't create too many rentals in one neighborhood.

Good neighborhoods are also distinctive for what they don't have. Good neighborhoods will have easy access to main streets and freeways, but they won't be too close to them. Good neighborhoods won't be near high-power lines, public utility plants, sewage treatment plants, or public dumps. Good neighborhoods should be near good schools, but not next to them.

PAUSE

Main Features of a Good Neighborhood

- Safe
- Good schools (not necessarily the best)
- Convenient shopping
- Majority of homes owned by residents
- Composed primarily of single-family homes
- Quality duplexes, triplexes or fourplexes are okay if located in good neighborhoods
- Near freeway, but not next to it
- Near good schools, but not next to them
- NOT near a busy street
- NOT near high-power lines
- NOT near sewage treatment plant or public dump

One caveat is: don't get hung up on buying in a neighborhood that is **too good**. We are buying rental homes and it's important for the prices to be low enough and the rents high enough for the investment to make sense. Buying homes that are too expensive usually does not work. Don't be too keen on getting the very best schools or the higher-end neighborhoods. Nice, in the middle of the quality spectrum, good, clean. No need to go for fancy.

Looking at Properties

Once you've chosen a market and selected the neighborhood(s) where you want to invest, you'll begin looking at properties on an individual basis. Sometimes investors—especially first-timers—get a little "hung up" at this juncture, because they use the same standards for a rental property as they would for a property they might live in. When you work with me and my staff, you will receive properties our brokers in the various markets have selected. Even so, I always recommend traveling to the market, meeting the broker and the property manager, and seeing the properties. Of course, during the 2020 COVID-19 pandemic, traveling became more of a challenge, so more video was used.

Thinking a rental property should follow what you prefer for your own home (especially when taken to the extreme) can be a mistake. There's nothing wrong with liking the property you purchase, and occasionally, when two properties are essentially the same, a choice will be made on aesthetics alone. Generally, however, it's best to set aside your likes and dislikes regarding architecture, interior design and landscaping. Most renters won't make their decision based on whether the house is Spanish-style or traditional, the carpet is tan or taupe, or whether there are roses or daisies in the garden—and neither should you. Your investment property will be a successful rental primarily because of three things:

- **Right location**
- **Right size**
- **Right price**

And those are the things you, as an investor, should look for, too. Of course, I'm assuming you're looking only at quality homes in good condition. When you invest in a quality home in the right location (good neighborhood) that's the right size (three bedrooms and two baths minimum), and rents for the right price (in line with comparable rentals in the same area), then you've just purchased a successful rental, regardless of whether you think the bathroom wallpaper is a bit old fashioned or wish the master bedroom was bigger.

I generally recommend new investors steer clear of homes with swimming pools. Although they do add value to the property and make it attractive to the tenant, I believe the drawbacks outweigh the benefits. Swimming pools are a danger to families with small children. They require a lot of maintenance and, in some states, require special fencing. This adds to your expenses and increases your potential liability.

 **PAUSE**

Important Features of a Winning Rental

- Quality home in good neighborhood
- Good schools
- 3-bedroom, 2-bath minimum
- Attached, 2-car garage
- Well-tended, low-maintenance yard
- Fenced backyard
- No swimming pool
- Easy access to good shopping
- Near major employers

The Rule of Conformity: When "Average" is Good

If you're not looking for any extra-special features, what should you look for?

What you really want is an average house in a good neighborhood full of good homes. The rule of conformity means: to get the most value from your property, it should conform to the standards set by most homes in the neighborhood.

Your investment property should be similar in style, size, condition and age to the houses surrounding it. Furthermore, it should be similar in price. Ideally, the purchase price will approximate—or be lower than—the median price for the area.

The Benefits of New Homes

Buying a brand-new home—or one that's about to be built—offers many nifty advantages for investors.

The first is, of course, the house is new, and everything is (or should be) in perfect condition. If there are any flaws, they'll be repaired under the homebuilder's warranty. You won't have to worry about repairs and refurbishments for at least the first few years. There's no need to paint, put in new wallpaper or new carpet. For busy investors, new homes are a godsend.

The second is, because you're buying the house knowing it will be a rental property, you can select the floor coverings, finishes, and appliances that will work best in a rental home. You'll want to choose neutral colors and durable (but not pricey) floor coverings, and appliances that can withstand the wear and tear of tenant turnover. Keeping an eye toward utility—not cosmetic beauty—will keep your initial costs down and minimize future replacement costs.

You can also choose a low-maintenance landscaping style. In some hot Sun Belt areas this often means using drought-resistant plants and a drip system. Tenants aren't always avid gardeners, and a low-maintenance yard will reduce the need for a landscape service, while keeping the yard attractive.

A third bonus is you can negotiate with builders for added amenities. We usually give builders a significant volume of sales when our investors and I buy through our local brokers, making everyone a "large client" (even if they just bought one home). This, in some cases, allows our local brokers to eke out extra benefits for our investors. Often the price of new homes is fixed, but builders are willing to offer upgrades such as a tile entry or an appliance package at no extra cost. Also, builders are often more willing than private owners to structure a deal that benefits you.

The fourth, and perhaps most intriguing benefit, is you can earn equity before you've closed escrow. How? Purchasing a new home occurs in two stages. First, you sign a contract with the builder and make an earnest money deposit of a few thousand dollars. You don't have to come up with the down payment until the house is completed, usually months later. In the Sun Belt regions we've discussed, in today's markets, often the property value rises between signing and closing. Many investors have purchased homes that have appreciated a couple of percentage points in less than six months.

Very importantly, new homes define the concept of a good neighborhood. Where new homes are built, new schools and shopping centers may be built, or already exist nearby as well. Some new home developments are part of a master-planned community with amenities such as parks, swimming pools, softball and soccer fields, and walking trails: just the kind of place where most families want to live.

It is not a strict law that buying new homes is best. During the recession (between 2008 and 2011) the best strategy was to buy foreclosed properties from the banks, at low values, regardless of what their age might have been. If you have a 1031 tax deferred exchange (outlined in Chapter 12), the time limits will likely not allow you to wait for new homes to be built. In that case, however, there are new homes that are ready to close now or in a couple of months at any given time. They would satisfy the exchange time requirements.

Analyzing Your Potential Investment Property, or Making the Numbers Work

Before you make an offer on a house, you'll want to be certain it will be a good investment. You do this by preparing a cash flow analysis of the property, or what I call "making the numbers work."

Before you can analyze the property, you must ask your realtor or property manager to supply you with answers to these questions:

- What will the property rent for?
- Is there a homeowner's association in the neighborhood?

   What are the monthly dues?
- What is the fee for property management?
- What is the annual property tax for this property?

Essentially, a cash flow analysis is a summary of monthly income (rent) minus monthly expenses (mortgage principal and interest, PMI (if any), taxes, insurance, property management fees and homeowner's association dues).

Following are two examples taken from actual properties in the Oklahoma City area.

PROPERTY #1

Sale Price:	$170,000
Down payment and closing costs:	$40,000
Mortgage:	$136,000 (30-year fixed @ 5%)
Monthly rent rate:	$1,350 to $1,450
Principal and interest:	$730
Taxes:	$161
Insurance:	$65
PMI:	$0
Property Management:	$112
Homeowner's Association:	$20
TOTAL:	**$983**
Monthly cash flow: +$262 to +$362	

PROPERTY #2

Sale Price:	$153,500
Down payment and closing costs:	$36,500
Mortgage:	$122,400 (30 yr. fixed @ 5%)
Monthly rent rate:	$1,225 to $1,325
Principal and interest:	$657
Taxes:	$44
Insurance:	$60
PMI:	$0
Property Management:	$102
Homeowner's Association:	$20
TOTAL:	**$983**
Monthly cash flow: +$242 to +$342	

As I mentioned before, I am using an interest rate of 5%, despite interest rates for investors currently (end of 2020) being about 3.4%. This is because the current rates are the lowest in history, and may not sustain for a long time. 5% may cover a longer period of relevance into the future. However, using 3.4% will improve the cash flow numbers in the examples.

As you can see from the examples, the cash flow analyses for the two properties show a positive monthly cash flow. Of course, these sheets only display the known factors. The unknown and potential issues are vacancies and repairs. For new homes, repairs are usually minimal for quite a while. Vacancy rates in Oklahoma City, as of this writing (2020), are under 3% (yes, this is a very strong rental market). I like to take about $150/month off for unexpected factors, and there is also a leasing fee charged one time when the property is vacant and gets rented, as well as a potential small yearly renewal fee (based on the management company). I account for these in the $150/month I subtract. This lowers the cash flow, but still leaves it positive. Does this mean the numbers don't work? On the contrary. The properties analyzed above are examples of investments that *do* work. Remember three things:

These properties have been leveraged quite a bit, with low down payments of 20%. Using a larger down payment will reduce the size of the mortgage, the monthly principal and interest payment, which will produce a higher positive cash flow.

The mortgage payment is fixed and will never change! Rents, however, are likely to continue increasing over the years with the cost of living, thus cash flow will improve.

Tax benefits have not been factored in.

Analyzing Your After-Tax Cash Flow

Although the Tax Reform Act of 1986 imposed stricter limitations on losses from real estate investments, and the Tax Law of 2018 retained a lot of these restrictions, you can still benefit from the favored status the government bestows on real estate investors. Along with deductions for repairs, travel and other expenses incurred from your rental activities, don't forget about the just-for-tax-purposes loss you can take against your property.

Cost Recovery, or Depreciation

Depreciation, also known as cost recovery, is a deduction the government allows you to take to recover the cost of an investment property that has a life beyond the tax year. For residential rental property, depreciation is deducted over a 27.5-year period.

However, only a certain portion of the property's cost can be depreciated. The amount eligible for depreciation is known as the improvement value, which is the cost of the property minus the value of the land.

To determine the improvement value of the property, you'll need to consult your tax preparer, realtor or appraiser. Although home building costs are relatively consistent throughout the country (save for very expensive areas where wages are very high and construction costs can be quite high as well), the price of land varies greatly from region to region. Real estate prices are often determined by land values. In states such as California, the value of the land has driven real estate prices so high.

This brings me to another reason why I choose to buy investment property in the Sun Belt. The cost of land is relatively low, so the improvement value is high in relation to the total cost of the property.

For example, let's compare two similar homes, one in California and one in Oklahoma. An average three-bedroom, two-bath house in the San Francisco Bay Area costs approximately $850,000 (depending on the source). Land in the Bay Area is so expensive that the improvement value of the property could easily be around $425,000, or only 50% of the total price. In Oklahoma City, a three-bedroom, two-bath house may sell for $170,000. Because land in Oklahoma City is less expensive than in the Bay Area, the Oklahoma City property will likely have an improvement value of $136,000, or 80% of the total price.

Land in the San Francisco Bay Area is expensive because the Bay Area is perceived as a great place to live and work, and so the demand for housing exceeds the supply. But if this perception of the Bay Area as a great place to live were to change—for instance, if there was a massive earthquake, or the recent yearly fires that have been raging—then the value of the land would decrease, and very possibly cause a significant decrease in home values.

In other words, there's a lot of "air" between the perceived value of the Bay Area property and its intrinsic value. That makes it much more vulnerable to economic and other fluctuations. Whereas the property in Oklahoma City is less volatile, because it has a greater intrinsic value, and a lot less "air" between its perceived and its intrinsic value.

When the improvement value of a property is high, the property is less vulnerable to economic downturns. It also means you will be able to depreciate a greater percentage of the property's overall value, and your depreciation deduction will go further toward offsetting your tax liability. In markets where land is at a premium, your depreciation deduction will not benefit you as much as in markets where the cost of land is lower.

How Depreciation is Calculated

Here's an example of how depreciation, or cost recovery, is calculated. Let's assume that Property #1 has an improvement value of $136,000. The deduction on a residential investment property with an improvement value of $136,000 is $4,945 per year, for 27.5 years. Let's also assume

the property rents at the low end, for $1,350 per month, and produces an annual cash flow of $3,144 ($262*12). When you subtract your depreciation deduction of $4,945, you can claim a loss of $1,801. If you're in the 32% tax bracket, that's a tax savings of $576, or an added "positive cash flow" of $48 per month. This is only for the federal tax portion. There is possibly an additional tax benefit at your state level. Of course, this assumes your Adjusted Gross Income dips well under $150,000, and you can deduct the losses from depreciation in that year. If not, the losses carry forward.

Property #2 has an improvement value of $122,800 and rents for $1,225 a month, producing a positive annual cash flow of $2,904 ($2,42*12). On a property with an improvement value of $122,800, the depreciation deduction is $4,465. After subtracting your profits ($2,904), you still have a tax loss of $1,561. If you're in the 32% tax bracket, this leads to a tax savings of $499. When you add the profits and tax savings together, you've made a total of $3,403 for the year; that's a positive cash flow of $284 per month, before unexpected expenses (which are also tax deductible).

As rental prices rise, your positive cash flow will increase, yet the depreciation deduction will help keep your taxable profits low.

Although I think the two properties analyzed above are perfect examples of good investments, keep in mind that by putting more money down, you'll have a higher positive cash flow, and you can use the profit to pay off the loan sooner. Remember, though, positive cash flow is not the Holy Grail of real estate investing. It's also important to look at how much you have to spend in order to make the investment.

Making an Offer:
Tips on Negotiating a Purchase Price

I like a good deal as much as the next guy. But when it comes to buying a quality single-family home investment property, a good deal usually means paying fair market value, or, if things go well, slightly less. In this case, it doesn't mean getting a "steal."

When you buy a quality home in a quality neighborhood in a quality market, you aren't going to have as much "wiggle room" on the price as you will when be buying low quality properties in bad markets. It's important to remember that you're investing in your future, not trying to "make a killing" overnight.

That said, there are things you can do to get a fair and reasonable price on an investment property. First, make sure your realtor is cognizant of comparable sales in the neighborhood and knows the fair market value of the property. He or she should be able to counsel you on the best offer to make and, if it's close to the fair market value, you can consider it a good deal. Note: "fair" means fair to both seller and buyer. Some real estate investors, however, insist on bidding under the seller's asking price simply because it makes them feel better about buying property if they feel they're getting a "deal."

While there's nothing wrong with doing this, you do take the chance your offer will fall on deaf ears. If you've found a property you think is a good investment, and it meets all the criteria, you might not want to take that chance.

Never forget you're making a long-term investment. Don't blow it just because the seller won't drop the price $2,000 or $3,000. That money's going to be financed over 30 years, after all, and represents only $400 or $600 out of your pocket. Fifteen years into the future, when the property might be worth twice what you paid for it, will you care if you paid $170,000 or $173,000? Most likely you won't—you'll just be glad you bought it. And likely lament not buying more (this is what I have been hearing for over 30 years now—from everyone!)

Negotiating with Builders

Buying new homes does offer some advantages when negotiating the purchase price. More than individual owners, new home builders are comfortable structuring a deal with a few bells and whistles. For instance, they're sometimes agreeable to cover all or part of the closing costs by adding it to the purchase price, which will cut down on the amount of cash you'll have to pay up front.

A good time to negotiate with home builders is near the end of the fiscal year, or when they're at the end of a subdivision. At all times, however, they are usually willing to offer amenity incentives: things that increase the value of the property but don't increase the price. For example, they may offer a better lot, backyard landscaping, appliances or upgraded carpet. Sometimes builders will entice you to use their lender, but you'll want to be cautious about this. In many cases the builder's lender will have higher loan fees than a lender you would find on your own. Be sure you check and do your due diligence before committing yourself.

Over the past few decades, it has become abundantly clear that using our brokers and property managers for my own purchases—as well as my investors'—pays great dividends. Even though each person buys his or her own homes in his or her name, we all appear to the service providers (brokers, property managers, builders) as one very large client. They know that if we have bought 1000 homes in their market over the past decade, and if even one of our investors who bought just one home is not happy, they risk losing 1000 homes. Thus, the investor who bought just one home still enjoys the clout stemming from 1000 homes. We have found over and over that instead of you reinventing the wheel, you can use the same brokers and managers I use myself and enjoy the greater power of the group (including me and my team looking over the service providers' shoulders). It won't solve all the universe's problems, but it sure helps. Especially if you are a busy person (as most of you are), buying homes by using the infrastructure we have already created in various markets brings you huge time savings, brokers who know what we are looking for and where to find it, and property managers eager to please a large group of owners.

What Happens During Escrow and Closing

Once the offer is signed between you and the seller, the contract and your earnest money deposit are delivered to an escrow officer at a title company, who will oversee the exchange of money and property.

Escrow officers work for escrow firms or title companies and are disinterested third parties who guarantee both you and the seller are treated fairly. They prepare documents related to the transfer of title, order a title search, and work with lenders for the transfer of funds. They're in charge of making sure all documents are signed and delivered, and the transfer of title is made public record.

After the escrow officer receives your contract, he or she will write a set of escrow instructions that is sent to you and the seller. The instructions include the date escrow is scheduled to close and any contingencies or conditions of sale affecting the transaction.

Contingencies ensure you can cancel the sale if stated conditions are not met. For example, if the property inspection report reveals structural or other damage, if you don't qualify for a loan, or if the title search uncovers unexpected liens or judgements.

During escrow, you'll receive a preliminary title report showing who currently owns the property, along with claims against the property such as mortgages, tax assessments, or income tax judgements. The current owner is required to clear the title of liens and judgements before the close of escrow.

Escrow is the time when you'll conduct a property inspection and obtain homeowner's insurance for the property (in fact, your escrow officer will prompt you to get it—escrow can't close on a financed property until you're properly insured). If your loan has not already been approved, you'll be working with the escrow officer and the lender to get your funding in place.

Once your loan is approved, the title is clear, and all contingencies to the sale have been resolved, escrow "closes" (the lender sends funds to the escrow company for transfer to the seller, and the transfer of title is recorded in the County Recorder's office). You'll receive a final "settlement statement" listing the money you deposited in escrow (your initial deposit, down payment and mortgage loan), and the funds paid out of escrow on your behalf (the total amount paid to the seller, loan fees, title fees, property inspection fees).

At all times during the escrow process, your realtor should be available to answer any questions or concerns you have. They've been through the process many times and should be in constant communication with your escrow officer. Good realtors can be extremely helpful with resolving issues between you and the seller and can help the escrow proceedings move along efficiently.

REPLAY

Buy in markets with the five essential criteria:

► Big City

► Good Rental Market Where the Numbers Work

► Not a Booming Market

► Low Median Price

► Sun Belt

► Good neighborhoods are composed primarily of single-family homes.

► Good neighborhoods have good schools, are safe, clean and convenient to shopping centers.

► The location, size, and price of your investment home matter more than the aesthetics.

► New homes have many benefits for investors.

CHAPTER 9

LET THE PROS MANAGE IT: RENTING YOUR PROPERTY

Scenario number one: you've just purchased an investment property, and you decide to manage it yourself. First, you've got to find a tenant. You post a "For Rent" sign on the lawn, place advertisements online, or maybe even in the local newspapers, and spend much more time answering emails and phone calls than you anticipated. You meet with prospective tenants, make sure they've filled out the rental application completely, and spend more time checking their references and talking to former landlords. Once you've narrowed the field, you run credit checks through a credit reporting service at $25 a pop.

Finally, after a month or two, you've found a tenant. You sigh with relief, thinking that the hard part's over. But too often, for too many landlords, the work's just begun.

First, the water heater quits. Next, little Susie flushes her Barbie down the toilet, or little Jimmie decides to see what happens after he drops a half-dozen marbles in the kitchen sink and turns on the disposal. A winter storm blows off a few roof tiles. The kids next door break a window playing baseball. A pipe bursts. The bathtub faucet leaks. The rain gutters need cleaning. A broken tile in the foyer must be replaced. The tree in the front yard needs a trim.

It's true that all homes need the occasional repair, and if you're already a homeowner, this list of troubles might not faze you. The difference between your own home and your rental property, however, is that repairs to your rental must be taken care of immediately, regardless of when they occur (the worst things always seem to happen at three a.m., or while you're on vacation). You may not mind going without hot water for three days, but by law, your tenant is entitled to a hotel stay if the hot water or heat is non-functional.

Until you manage a rental property yourself, you might not realize how much of your time and effort is required to make these repairs. And I'm not talking about doing it yourself. Simply finding the necessary contractors, negotiating prices, and arranging dates and times convenient to both the contractor and the tenant takes a considerable amount of time. Then, of course, you've got to make sure the work was done properly.

If the rent payment is late, you'll have to deal with the tenant on an issue that is bound to be stressful to both of you. When the tenant moves out, it's up to you to determine the amount of the security deposit refund: whether the tenant's toll on your property is the result of normal wear and tear, or if excessive wear will require you to withhold some of the deposit. This problem, more than any other, is what brings landlords and tenants together in small claims court. That's another big chunk of your time, not to mention the unpleasantness of it all.

And, of course, when your present tenant moves out, you'll have to start all over again...getting the property in move-in condition, advertising, taking phone calls, interviewing prospective tenants, and conducting background checks.

If you have time, patience, and a good sense of humor ("Please tell little Susie how sorry I am to hear that only Barbie's head survived the tragic accident") managing your investment properties might work for you. But I suspect that, like most of us, your life is already full to the bursting point. Does that mean you can't own investment property? Not at all. Which brings me to...

Scenario number two: You've just purchased an investment home and have hired a property management company that specializes in the management of single-family residences. What happens next? Very, very little. At most, you'll approve the tenant they've chosen and sign the lease.

What about repairs? Late payments? Cleaning deposit refunds? The property manager is there to handle everything, from advertising the rental and screening tenants, to hiring contractors and overseeing the repair work...and more. You won't have to do much more than approve (or not approve) any repair expenses. You'll never get a phone call at three a.m., or while you're on vacation (unless you've specifically asked the property manager to contact you).

In most cases, when you hire a property manager, your investment will require only a little of your time via the occasional email or phone call. For me, there's no contest between the two scenarios. If you're busy, property management is the only way to go.

An even better way: I have learned, over a few decades investing full time in single-family rental homes, and helping many thousands worldwide do the same, that the original way we did it when I began in Las Vegas in the 1980s is even better. I led a group of Silicon Valley engineers and we bought over 250 homes in a couple of years. Even though each person bought their own homes in their name, we still appeared to the service providers (property management firm, broker, repair crews), to be one very large client. Even the engineer who bought just one home wielded the clout that came from over 250 homes. If that owner was not happy with anything the manager did and complained to me, once I called the manager on his behalf, the manager heard "250 homes talking." The manager knew they could lose all 250 homes if I was unhappy with them, not to mention the many future homes we might have bought and given them to manage. This way everyone enjoyed more clout with the managers.

To this day, we use this same model. In Phoenix we have bought over 3,000 homes. In Oklahoma City over 1,700, in Orlando over 1,000 and so on in many other cities. Using the same property managers I use for my own properties, and that all ICG investors also use, creates an extra layer of clout, which benefits all investors, big or small.

Especially for busy people, this makes life even easier. Of course, this doesn't solve all the problems in the universe, but having this extra clout is always welcome. It also saves the busy investor time, since the property management firm had already been identified and tested before they even bought their first home.

What Property Managers Do

A full-service property management company has four coordinating functions: people (tenant screening); financial (rent collection and disbursement, accounting services); construction (maintenance and repair); and legal (lease agreements, eviction proceedings). They are responsible for renting and managing your property in all its aspects, and will offer these services:

- Advertising and marketing
- Property showing
- Tenant screening, including credit checks and background checks
- Lease negotiation
- Rent collection
- Repair coordination and oversight
- Property inspection
- Monthly and annual accounting
- Lease renewal
- Tenant negotiation
- Eviction services

After you sign on with a property management company, they determine the monthly rental rate based on comparable rentals in the surrounding area. The property manager then advertises the rental, using all the means at their disposal, including signage, web-based advertising, and multiple listing services, if needed.

The property management company will show the property, collect tenant applications, conduct tenant interviews and credit checks and review the rental history of potential tenants. They will offer recommendations on the best tenant for your property. After the lease agreement is signed, the property management company will make sure that your rental property is in move-in condition.

Each month the property management company will collect rent from your tenant. The check will be deposited in a large trust account in which you, the property owner, have a separate account. You are paid by the property management company out of this trust account.

The property management company will keep you apprised of any necessary repairs and will coordinate the repairs by contacting tenants to arrange times for vendors or repairmen to come by. Often, property managers work with a select group of contractors with whom they've negotiated discount pricing.

The property manager understands the state and local landlord-tenant laws. This is extremely important if any problems arise with your tenant. A good property manager can help you stay out of small claims court and knows how to conduct a tenant eviction so that it's effective yet abides by state and local laws.

An important part of property management occurs when there's a tenant turnover. A difficult aspect of rental management is distinguishing normal wear and tear on a property from excess wear. The property manager knows how to tell the difference and how to determine the correct amount of the deposit refund. They can help you avoid any disputes over this issue, which is often a troublesome one for property owners.

Benefits to You, the Property Owner

Just as your stock portfolio or 401(k) is managed by someone who is familiar with the stock market, property managers are asset managers. They have vast experience working with many property owners and many tenants and can do much to promote the profitability of your property. They can also help you avoid the problems that sometimes accompany property ownership. When you use a property manager you don't have to screen tenants, collect rent, advertise or hire contractors. In addition, property managers can protect your anonymity, if you prefer being anonymous.

The primary benefit to using a property manager is that it saves you time. You don't have to be an active landlord, or learn the many skills involved in successfully managing your property (and too often novice real estate investors learn the hard way, through costly mistakes). The monthly and annual statements prepared by the property management company will make your bookkeeping tasks much easier, with your income and expenses already calculated, ready to be entered into your tax returns.

Cost of Property Management

Property management companies charge a percentage, usually somewhere between eight percent and nine percent, of the gross rent collected. For a house that rents for $1400 a month, at 8% the property management fee would be $112 per month. Their fee is deducted monthly from the rental income, before a check is issued to the property owner. Most management companies also charge a "leasing fee," which is typically charged only when the property is vacant and gets rented. This fee is usually expressed as a percentage of one month's rent (I have seen 50%-100%), and it covers all showings of the home, all credit report pulling on prospective tenants, employment verification, interviewing current & past landlords (if relevant), and being able to pay other brokers a commission if they bring a tenant.

Some property managers also charge a small fee on annual renewal, but many don't. That fee reflects certain activities and protocols that the manager performs upon renewal.

Selecting a Property Management Company

As I said above, the best way to go is use the property management firm already established and used as part of the infrastructure of a large group of investors, such as the group of our investors, which ICG has been helping for decades. This way, as discussed above, you not only use a property management firm who has already been used by other investors, but you enjoy the clout that comes from being a large client, by virtue of being an investor in our universe, and knowing that the managers are eager to please me and my company so they can retain the large volume of business of which you are a part.

You can find property management companies on the web under "Real Estate Management." Another good source is the National Association of Residential Property Managers (NARPM) website at narpm.org, which offers a search feature of property managers by region. This association of thousands of property managers requires members to have a tested level of professional skill and to abide by a code of ethics.

Narrow the field first by selecting only full-time property management firms. This means no part-time or side-line property managers; often real estate offices or other real estate professionals will advertise themselves as property managers, sometimes offering a cut-rate fee. As in most things in life, you pay for what you get, and slip-shod management can be worse than no management at all. What you want is a management company that will be available 24 hours a day, if necessary, and one that will manage your asset on every front, from showing and renting to repairs and maintenance.

Important Questions to Ask Potential Property Managers

How long have you been in business?

The longer, the better, of course. Experience counts.

Are you a member of any professional associations?

The National Association of Residential Property Managers (NARPM) and the Property Managers Association (PMA) are two professional associations that require management companies to abide by professional standards and practices.

Do you specialize in residential properties?

You want a management company that either specializes or deals only in residential management. Companies that specialize in commercial property management (office buildings, etc.) may not understand your or your tenant's needs.

Do you work weekends?

A good property management company is available to oversee your property 24 hours a day, seven days a week.

How many properties do you currently manage?
What is the total number of properties you've managed?

As above, experience counts...just be sure they have the staff necessary to handle their clientele.

Are these properties in the same area or neighborhood as my property?

Knowledge of the neighborhood in which your property is located is preferred. This means that the property management company will know the type and age of your property, and comparable rentals. They'll also be familiar with the neighborhood homeowner's association.

Can you provide references?

Ask for the names and numbers of a few other property owners who have properties similar to yours. Don't hesitate to call them and ask if they've been satisfied by the service they've received from the management company. Using the management company we already use for myself and our ICG investors, you also have our experience with the managers to use as a reference.

Which services do you offer?

Make sure that the management company offers all the services listed above.

What is your fee?

Somewhere between seven and ten (eight to nine is most common, as I mention above) percent of the gross rent collected is the standard throughout the industry, as is a fee for leasing. Keep in mind that you may be able to negotiate a lower fee than what the management company is asking for, especially if you have multiple properties. At ICG, we usually lower the rates from ten to eight percent. We COULD lower it more, but it is also important for the managers to be paid adequately so they can run their business well.

Do you charge a leasing fee?

A leasing fee is quite common and is usually for an amount equal to between one-half to one month's rent. It covers advertising costs, fees to other managers for bringing in tenants from an MLS listing, credit checks and other expenses associated with qualifying tenants, showing the property, etc.

Do you have an additional fee for lease renewal?

In most cases, there is not a separate fee for lease renewal, if the leasing fee has been paid. Some managers do charge a small fee.

How do you advertise and market the properties you manage?

Excellent marketing skills are crucial to the profitability of your property. The management company you choose should advertise and market your property on multiple fronts: through the Multiple Listing Service (with many websites dedicated to rental, usage of the MLS is declining amongst property management firms), and web-based advertising, using the prevalent and well-known realty websites.

What is the average time for renting a new property?

The time it takes to rent your property often depends on the amount of rental activity in the market where your property is located. In the markets mentioned earlier in the book (Oklahoma City, Tampa, Baton Rouge etc.), residential properties can usually be rented in one to two months. Currently, in 2020, the average time to rent is under 45 days. If the management company quotes a longer period than that, find out why.

What is the average time to "turnaround" a property: cleaning, repairs, new tenant?

You're hiring a management company to help keep your property profitable. Be certain they have all the vendors (painters, carpet cleaners, etc.) necessary to keep turnaround time to a minimum.

How often do you check on the property?

The property manager who is assigned to your property should conduct periodic drive-by checks. Find out how often they intend to make a drive-by inspection and what they look for. Some managers charge a bit extra to do an interior inspection once a year or more. Ask about it.

Which vendors and contractors do you work with?

The management company could provide you with a list of their vendors and contractors: appliance dealers, plumbers, carpenters, landscape services, etc. Ask if the contractors are licensed and bonded. This may not be information the manager would want to freely share with you, as they do not want people to start using their vendor network outside of their business. They spent years developing their team, and it works best when used in the context of their management.

How do you handle late payments?

Generally, management companies collect rent on a specified day each month, the first or the fifth. If a rent payment is late, they will issue a late notice. You'll want to know if they have any special techniques or skills for dealing with late-paying tenants.

Have you ever evicted tenants? What is your procedure? What is the cost to the owner?

Evictions, of course, must follow the laws set down by the state in which your property is located. Ask the management company to explain the local eviction laws, and whether they have a legal department or attorney on retainer who will handle it. Of course, in most of the Sun Belt states, where we recommend investing, the eviction process is relatively fast and inexpensive, as opposed to states like New York and California.

Do you issue monthly and annual statements?

Accountability is an important feature of a good property management company. They should have computerized accounting which issues a monthly statement with income (rent payments) and expenses (management fee, repairs) clearly stated. In addition, an annual statement should reflect all monthly statements and any tax information you need for your tax return.

Once you've asked all these questions, you should know if the property management company is capable of taking care of all your needs. Then ask yourself how you feel about your conversation with them. Are they able to answer all your questions in detail? Is there any point on which you feel you've gotten less than a complete answer? How are their communications skills? One of the primary jobs of a property manager is dealing with tenants, and good communication is requisite.

How to Minimize Vacancies: Tips on Attracting and Keeping Good Tenants

First of all, what's a good tenant? The bottom line is, of course, one who pays the rent on time. Ask a few property owners and you'll come up with a wish list of other qualities: stays in the rental for years, never complains, keeps your property looking like a showplace, is an avid gardener, doesn't mind making minor repairs, is always available to open the house up for contractors, doesn't open an auto repair business on the front lawn or start fires in the kitchen.

This, however, is a dream tenant, and those are hard to come by. Happily, when you've got a good property manager, your peace of mind doesn't have to rely on an elusive dream tenant. A good tenant—one who's responsible and reasonable—will do just fine. Here are a few pointers that will help you attract good tenants and keep them.

Keep your property in excellent shape functionally and aesthetically.

When your investment property shows pride of ownership—clean, with a well-tended yard, fresh paint and spotless floor coverings—you're going to attract a better class of tenant.

Allow children and pets.

Remember, you're investing in single-family residences. Families have children. Families have pets. Yes, Fido and Fluffy might do a little damage to the carpets or the yard, but it's fixable. What's more important is that your tenant remains in the house for at least two or three years. Families with children and pets tend to settle in and stay awhile, especially if your property is in a good neighborhood, with good schools. A few square feet of carpet are much less costly than vacancies and tenant turnover.

Create low-maintenance yards or hire a gardening service.

No doubt your tenant is as busy as you are. And, like most of us, they probably don't have the time or the inclination to be out in the yard mowing, watering, and pruning every weekend.

Do yourself and them a favor by creating an easy-care yard with a drip system or hire a landscape service. In some hot weather Sun Belt areas, like Phoenix and Las Vegas, desert landscaping is a good bet. Desert landscaping usually consists of indigenous plants that need little or no water along with colored rocks and sand. It's attractive, with zero to low maintenance. In other markets, defer to the judgment of the broker and the property manager as to what kind of yard to have. Your tenants will appreciate coming home every night to a house with an attractive yard, and you'll know, without a doubt, that your property will always have curb-side appeal—and will look good for the next tenant.

Be respectful.

Your investment may be your property, but it's your tenant's home. They deserve a landlord who respects their privacy, is cognizant of their needs, and responsive to their problems. This doesn't mean you must be available to them day and night, but it is up to you to make sure their problems are being addressed promptly by the management company.

The Dos and Don'ts of Repairs and Renovations

The most common mistake I see among property owners, especially those who own single-family homes, is the tendency to impose their own aesthetic standards and values on their rental property.

For example, an investor from California purchased a single-family home in Arizona. In Arizona, electric kitchens are common. In California, it's the opposite: gas stoves are the norm, and considered more desirable than electric.

This investor decided that, to make his property more appealing, he would rip out the electric kitchen and install gas appliances. Three months and thousands of dollars later, he'd changed a perfectly good kitchen into one that suited his needs.

Did the house rent faster? No. Was he able to charge a higher rent? No. All the owner had done was reduce the profitability of his investment—and, in fact, the kitchen looked worse than before.

Over-improvement can be as detrimental to your investment's bottom line as neglecting the property. Repairs and renovations to rental properties should be based upon functionality, not aesthetics. Of course, you want your investment home to look nice, but it doesn't have to conform to your idea of beauty, or even convenience. Save that for the home you live in.

Good rental properties adhere to the standards set by similar rental properties in the surrounding neighborhood.

Necessary Repairs

When you buy a quality home in a good neighborhood, you won't have to worry much about major repairs. Houses less than 15 years old seldom need new foundations, new heating systems or extensive re-plumbing. The lack of major repair work is one of the many reasons why I recommend buying brand-new, high-quality properties. No matter what the age of your property, however, you'll want to make certain that all the items listed below are in perfect working order. Keep in mind, however, that you'll have a team—your property management company— to keep abreast of all this.

Roof

Composition roofs generally need to be replaced every 15-20 years. In some locations, newer homes may have tile roofs, which last a lot longer.

Foundation

Bad foundations cause stress on the structure, which leads to all kinds of problems: interior cracks, stuck doors and windows, roof problems, etc.

Garage Door

Whether it's manual or automatic, the garage door should open smoothly and easily. An automatic garage door is always preferable.

Driveway

Cracks in the driveway are unsightly and are a detriment to the "curb-side" appeal of your home. Small cracks left untended tend to become larger; weeds can grow in the cracks, forcing the concrete farther apart. It's best to take care of them early on.

Fences

Many states have fencing laws that must be adhered to. Having a broken or incomplete fence around your property can lead to lawsuits.

Heating and Cooling Systems

Thermostats, furnaces, and air vents should all be checked periodically. Often, the local gas and electric company will do a free inspection of the property's heating and cooling system, relight extinguished pilot lights, and check carbon monoxide levels.

Plumbing

Toilets, tubs, and showers should have strong water pressure and good drainage. Problems with toilet flushing can often be repaired by replacing the parts inside the toilet tank, especially is it's a relatively new toilet. Hot water heaters have an average life of 20 years; an occasional "flush" (draining so the sediment in the bottom is cleaned out) can help keep them working efficiently. If your tenants have children, you may want to keep the hot water temperature set below 110 degrees, to prevent accidental scalding.

Electrical

All outlets and light fixtures should be functional. Large appliances such as refrigerators, washers, dryers, and dishwashers should have grounded 220 electrical hookups.

Fireplace

The flue inside the fireplace should open and close smoothly, and smoke should draw easily. Brick and mortar fireplaces should be inspected for cracks or damage. A fireplace cover, such as one with sliding glass doors, reduces the possibility of accidents, fire, and reduces the amount of smoke and soot that gets into the house.

Appliances

All appliances should be clean and work efficiently. They don't have to be state-of-the-art but should look relatively new. Inspect washer and dishwasher for proper drainage and leaking. The clothes dryer must have adequate ventilation; dryer lint build-up is a fire hazard.

Floor Coverings

All carpeting, linoleum and tile should be clean and in good condition, without stains, holes, tears, or cracks. You don't have to carpet the entire house just because there are problems in one room; usually you can find carpet that will closely match the existing carpet.

Doors and Windows

Doors should be level, and able to close tightly. Windows should be without cracks in panes or sashes and should open easily.

Window Treatments

I usually have mini-blinds installed on the windows of my rental properties. They're inexpensive, yet look good from the house exterior, and provide a consistent look throughout the house. Curtains tend to be more expensive, and more prone to wear and tear.

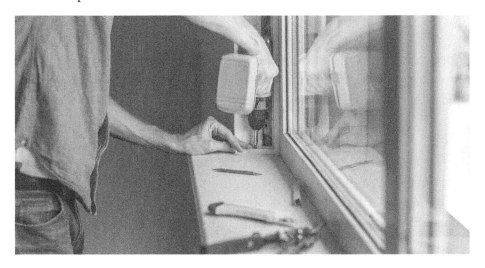

Smoke Alarms

Smoke alarms should be installed in each bedroom, the living room (especially if there's a fireplace), and in the kitchen. You may even want to add a small fire extinguisher in the kitchen, easily accessible in case someone's flambé gets out of hand. Smoke alarms should be checked periodically, and new batteries installed once a year. Check with your management company to make sure this is part of its oversight. Don't rely on your tenants to take care of this!

Security

Adequate security is as important to your tenant as it is to you. There should be deadbolts on both the front and back doors; sliding glass doors and windows should shut and lock securely.

Walls

Holes, cracks and water stains should be repaired. Marks or scratches can often be removed simply by cleaning, or paint touch-ups. Generally bedroom walls take the most abuse, especially if children live in the house. It's also common to paint before a new tenant moves in, unless the previous tenant was there for less than a year.

All the above are maintenance issues. Paying attention to them is important; keeping these things in good repair keeps your property functional, safe, and livable. When your property manager calls and tells you there's a problem with any of the above items, you need to listen. Ignoring the structural systems of your house will only make problems worse and will often lead to unhappy owner-tenant relations.

On the other hand, you are not required to make cosmetic changes or upgrades to please your tenant. These would include new paint or carpet, when the current paint and carpet is in good condition; wallpaper, new appliances, microwave ovens, additional landscaping, bay windows, patio covers, etc. It will help you to know what is considered standard for other rentals in the area; your property manager can help with this. And, in fact, he or she can help you make decisions about your property that are good business decisions, and not based on personal taste.

 **REPLAY**

- ► Personally managing your property is time-consuming.
- ► Although you can choose to make all final decisions, a property management company can save you time, costly mistakes, and help keep your investment profitable.
- ► Property management companies usually charge a fee of 7% to 10% of the gross rent collected, plus a leasing fee.
- ► It is recommended to use the property management firm already in use by many investors, such as ICG's investors. This serves to know their performance and to enjoy the clout of the whole group of investors as a "large client", even though you buy the house in your name.
- ► Good tenants are attracted to good properties and fair, responsible owners.
- ► Cosmetic changes or upgrades to your property are not cost-effective.

CHAPTER 10

BUILDING YOUR PORTFOLIO

One of the advantages of real estate is the ability to leverage your initial investment into further investments, thereby increasing your net worth and income.

Your ultimate goal should be to purchase multiple properties. How many properties you purchase depends on your needs and goals. When you buy quality single-family homes in good neighborhoods, and have them managed by professional property managers, the number of homes you can own is limited only by the capital at your disposal.

Setting Goals

Soon after you buy your first investment home—or even before—sit down with your spouse or significant other and discuss your life goals. If you don't have a significant other, you may want to confer with your CPA or tax advisor. There's something about talking about your goals that makes them more real and forces you to look at the reality of your current situation. It's one thing to have a recurring fantasy of quitting your job and sailing around the world; but once you say it out loud, your partner's either going to point out the complete unfeasibility of the idea or help create a plan to make it happen (hopefully, your spouse loves to sail, too). Talking about what you want from life will help you make decisions and commitments. The dreams that are never discussed are usually the ones that are never realized.

The first thing you should talk about is the age at which you want to retire. As with all long-term goals, this may change over the years; the important thing is to choose a number and set a goal. For most people, the golden age is still 65. However, these days, I have many investors only BEGINNING to build their portfolio for the future in their sixties or even at an older age. Life expectancy is rapidly increasing (especially due to technological breakthroughs). Even starting out in your sixties, it is likely you will need to build a solid retirement portfolio for when you are in your late seventies, and you will be very thankful you created this rental home portfolio, that will provide growth for your future and create lasting financial strength for the rest of your life, no matter how long you may live.

Even if you believe that you'll never retire, choose a number. As you grow older, you'll realize how important is it to invest for your later years. After all, even multi-millionaires can continue to work, if they want to. The difference between them and most people is that they have a choice.

Next, consider the annual income you'll need after retirement, or if you are already retired, the income you will need later in life. Remember, you only need to think in terms of today's dollars. If you were to retire today (or if you are already retired), how much income would you require each year? Finally, what financial hurdles do you face before retirement? Will you need to finance a college education, help provide for your parents' retirement, or would you like to start your own business? If you've already completed the steps in Chapter Six, you've got a good sense of your current financial picture and have begun putting aside investment funds. Now's the time to decide when you want to reach your goals and make a timeline for investing.

How to Estimate the Number of Properties You'll Need

Your retirement income will come from the rents received from your investment properties. Your goal is to own many homes free and clear—in other words, with the mortgage fully paid off—by the time you retire, or at a point in the future you designate if you are already retired. In Chapter 2, I explained how to estimate the monthly income from a rental property. I'll recap it here, with a reminder that we're talking in today's dollars: over the years, these figures will rise along with the cost of living.

A variation on this theme is to simply own homes with inflation-eroded fixed rate mortgages that may not have been completely paid off but are getting more insignificant every year. Such a variation may allow you to make smaller payments over the years, potentially buy more homes, and still let inflation chew away the real value of your loans deep into the future. In the examples in this chapter, I assume we are aiming for free and clear homes as our building blocks for the future.

On a $170,000 home that rents for $1,400 per month, there's a $850 per month profit once the mortgage is paid off. The other $550 goes toward recurring expenses, such as property tax, insurance, property management, vacancies and repairs. One free and clear home will net approximately $10,000 per year. You can see how quickly this adds up.

1 HOME	$10,000 per year
2 HOMES	$20,000 per year
3 HOMES	$30,000 per year
4 HOMES	$40,000 per year
5 HOMES	$50,000 per year
6 HOMES	$60,000 per year
7 HOMES	$70,000 per year
8 HOMES	$80,000 per year
9 HOMES	$90,000 per year
10 HOMES	$100,000 per year
15 HOMES	$150,000 per year
20 HOMES	$200,000 per year

Once you've decided on the amount of annual income you'd like to have upon retirement, create a plan for buying properties. If you can buy multiple properties right away, that's terrific—you'll be well on your way to a great financial future. But perhaps you can only buy one right now. If that's true, then it's essential to make a financial plan to buy more properties in the future—a plan that's truly doable for you, one that you can accomplish and live with.

Following are scenarios of three different couples. Each couple was at a different stage in life, had different goals and financial requirements, but each couple was able to use real estate as a financial planning tool.

The charts accompanying the scenarios use a constant home price of $170,000, financed with a 30-year, fixed rate loan at 5% interest with 20% down. All figures except for those in the very last line are calculated in today's dollars and have not been adjusted for inflation. The last line of

the chart shows the amount of the amassed equity and projected income as a future value; in other words, after the value of today's dollars has been adjusted for inflation.

John and Susan: Scenario #1

John and Susan, both age 38, initially purchased two homes that they intended to use to finance their children's college education. To build up equity faster, they made substantial additional principal payments each year to pay them off in 15 years (or, in this case, they could have opted for a 15-year loan to begin with). After fifteen years, there was enough equity in the homes so that refinancing would provide plenty of cash for college expenses.

Five years after buying their first two homes, John and Susan began buying homes for their retirement. At 43, they estimated that their retirement was twenty-two years away, so extra principal payments on these homes so they are paid off at age 65 were very minimal. The income and the tax savings from their first two rental properties made it easier to save money each month. In fact, any profit after the extra principal payments were made, besides the small extra principal payments, was put into a money market account that was used to help save for a down payment on another property. In this way, they could buy one more property each year.

SCENARIO #1 JOHN & SUSAN			
Age		**Gross Equity**	**Cash Assets/ Income**
38	Purchased 2 homes	$68,000	
43	Began buying 1 home per year	$178,631	
53	2 homes free & clear + 10 homes with various amounts of equity	$788,018	
53	Refinanced first 2 homes (70% 2 new loans of $119,000 each)	$550,018	$238,000 (lump sum)
65	10 homes free & clear + 12 years of equity build-up in first 2 homes	$1,764,307 (today's $)	$100,000 income per yr (today's $)
FUTURE VALUE AT AGE 65: (with estimated 3% annual inflation)		$3,186,535 Equity	$191,610 Annual Income

All figures except for those in the very last line are calculated in today's dollars and have not been adjusted for inflation. The last line of the chart shows the amount of the amassed equity and projected income as a future value; in other words, after the value of today's dollars has been adjusted for inflation. Refinance expenses omitted just for simplification.

By age 53, they owned 12 houses: 2 that were refinanced to provide for their children's education, and 10 that were held for their retirement. By age 65, they owned 10 houses free and clear, along with the first 2 houses they had purchased, which had built up another 12 years of equity.

As you can see from the above figures, John and Susan started out with a relatively low investment, approximately $70,000. By reinvesting their rental income and adding to it with their savings, they could pay off the first 2 houses in 15 years and buy more houses. So, beginning with $70,000 they could pay for two four-year university stints (likely in a good state university), have a retirement income of $100,000 a year (in today's dollars), and own real property with a value of over $1.75 million (in today's dollars). There are some additional details like closing costs, loan costs etc. However, I chose to simplify the scenario in order to illustrate the big picture.

Julie and Michael: Scenario #2

Julie and Michael, in their fifties, had already set aside money for their children's education. Most of all, they needed to plan for their retirement, which they estimated was 15 years in the future, since they both planned to retire around age 69, knowing full well about the ever-increasing lifespans due to technological advances (which we discussed in Chapter 1), and feeling that working a couple of extra years may help launch a carefree retirement for a long time to follow, especially harnessing the power of single-family home rentals. In addition, Julie hoped to someday change careers and start her own business.

They began by buying six homes, with five earmarked for retirement. The sixth house, which they planned to pay off in ten years, was set aside to finance Julie's business. Escalating rents and decent mortgage interest rates made it possible to pay off the homes in 15 years—and for Julie and Michael to get over $130,000 when they refinanced the sixth house only ten years after buying it. In this way, Julie could launch the business that she'd always dreamed of, without jeopardizing their retirement income.

SCENARIO #2 JULIE & MICHAEL			
Age		**Gross Equity**	**Cash Assets/ Income**
54	Purchased 6 homes	$204,000	
64	1 homes free & clear + 10 homes with various amounts of equity	$735,048	
64	Refinanced free & clear home (1 new loan of $136,000)	$599,048	$136,000
69	5 homes free & clear + 5 years of equity build-up in first home	$918,602 (today's $)	$50,000 per year (today's $)
FUTURE VALUE AT AGE 65: (with estimated 3% annual inflation)		$1,431,151 Equity	$77,898 Annual Income

All figures except for those in the very last line are calculated in today's dollars and have not been adjusted for inflation. The last line of the chart shows the amount of the amassed equity and projected income as a future value; in other words, after the value of today's dollars has been adjusted for inflation. Refinance expenses omitted just for simplification.

Lisa and Lowell: Scenario #3

Lisa and Lowell, in their sixties, had less time to plan for their retirement than the two previous couples. However, being older, they had more cash available, and used it to make larger down payments on the 8 homes they purchased. They were also keenly aware of how, even though they were both 63 years old, the day might come when they are both 78 years old (and likely in good health, as they were avid fitness buffs and ate cleanly). They knew that if they did not take action at 63, they would likely greatly regret it at age 78 (with a statistical long life still ahead of them as we discussed in Chapter 1). Larger down payments meant smaller mortgages and higher profits from rental income. They used their profits to pay off the homes in fifteen years: at age 78, they owned property worth over one and a quarter million (in today's dollars) which generated an annual income of $80,000 (in today's dollars).

SCENARIO #3 LISA & LOWELL

Age		Gross Equity	Cash Assets/ Income
63	Purchased 8 homes with 30% down	$408,000	
78	8 homes free & clear	$1,360,000	
FUTURE VALUE AT AGE 65: (with estimated 3% annual inflation)		$2,118,836 Equity	$107,513 Annual Income

All figures except for those in the very last line are calculated in today's dollars and have not been adjusted for inflation. The last line of the chart shows the amount of the amassed equity and projected income as a future value; in other words, after the value of today's dollars has been adjusted for inflation. Refinance expenses omitted just for simplification.

 **REPLAY**

- ► Purchasing multiple properties as "building blocks" should be your goal.
- ► Discuss your life goals and make a commitment to attaining them.
- ► Choose an age at which you'd like to retire, or a target age if you are already retired.
- ► Estimate the number of properties you'll need. Create a timeline for purchasing properties.
- ► It is never too late to start. Starting in your sixties will pay great dividends in your seventies.

CHAPTER 11

KEEPING TRACK OF YOUR INVESTMENTS

Even when you own multiple properties, there's a simple system for charting income, expenses and other essential money-related issues that requires only a little of your time. For those who are computer-savvy, I've included some information on using Quicken® as your accounting system. Quicken is very simple to use. However, many accountants would prefer that you use QuickBooks, which is a more complete accounting software, but you can even get the job done with nothing more than a spreadsheet, a pencil, some paper, and a calculator.

Before you begin looking at the bottom line, however, you'll need to do two things: open a checking account and create a filing system.

Set Up a Separate Checking Account

Treat your real estate investment as a business, and keep it separate from your personal affairs. I strongly suggest opening a separate checking account used solely for rent deposits mortgage payments, and other rental related income and expenses. Even if you only have one investment property, a separate account will help you keep track of investment income and expenses.

Organizing Documents

Purchasing property generates a lot of paper. If you've bought a house before, you already know about the tome-sized stack of documents you have to sign at closing. Included in this are the loan documents and various forms such as the Loan Estimate, Equal Opportunity Housing Act and Disclosure Statement.

Because the first (and the last) set of papers you'll keep are legal-size, I recommend buying a legal-size file cabinet, along with legal-size hanging files and manila file folders.

Create a Filing System

Each property should have its own separate hanging file, labeled with the property's address. Into this file goes that first sheaf of signed papers you brought home from the title company. Next, label a set of manila file folders with the following headings:

- **Rent Payments**
- **Mortgage Payments**
- **Property Management**
- **Mortgage Statements**
- **Repairs**
- **Taxes**
- **Insurance**
- **Travel**
- **Miscellaneous Expenses**

These file folders should be kept in an adjacent hanging file (or two, if necessary), listed with the property's address, and should contain documents relating only to that property. Each property you own will require a set of the file folders listed above.

For the first two file folders, **Rent** and **Mortgage Payments**, you'll need lined or graph paper to create a record of all transactions by month (or a printout of a spreadsheet, for example). If you owned the property for the entire year, begin with January. If you purchased the house later in the year, begin with the month in which you first paid the mortgage. For each month add these headings, left to right: Rent, Check Number, Date Deposited, Mortgage, Check Number, Date Paid, Profit/Loss.

A sample spreadsheet would look like this:

	RENT	CK#	DATE DEP.	MORT.	CK#	DATE PD.	P/L
Jan.							
Feb.	$,1400	226	2/7/18				$1,400
Mar.	$1,400	237	3/7/18	$730	431	3/15	$670
Apr.	$,1400	248	4/7/18	$730	485	4/15	$670
May	$,1400	256	5/7/18	$730	515	5/15	$670
Jun.	$,1400	278	6/7/18	$730	621	6/15	$670
Jul.	$,1400	301	7/7/18	$730	646	7/15	$670
Aug.	$1,400	322	8/7/18	$730	701	8/15	$670
Sep.	$1,400	345	9/7/18	$730	736	9/15	$670
Oct.	$1,400	369	10/7/18	$730	776	10/15	$670
Nov.	$1,400	384	11/7/18	$730	825	11/15	$670
Dec.	$1,400	410	12/7/18	$730	854	12/15	$670

In the above example, the property was purchased in January, and the first rental income was received in February. It's important to list all the months in which you paid the mortgage, not just the months in which you received rental income, so that you'll know how your expenses offset income at the end of the year. Since the property in this example was purchased in January, the prorated mortgage payment for January was made at the closing by the title company. The February payment will only be paid in March, as mortgage payments are made in arrears. Of course, in the example above we simplified the universe to only include rent and mortgage payments (principal and interest). Needless to say, in a real spreadsheet there would also be property taxes, insurance, management fees, and any repairs and other possible expenses. These were not shown here only so a clean picture is presented, but they always are there, of course.

If you have Excel, Google Docs or similar software, you can set up a spreadsheet that will calculate the profit or loss column for you (although a pencil and a calculator will do the job easily if you wish to go old school). Of course, accounting software like QuickBooks or the simpler version, Quicken (which may suffice for a few rental homes), will do the job very well.

Filing Records and Receipts

In the **Property Management** folder, you'll keep the monthly and annual statements issued by the property management company. In the **Mortgage Statements** folder, file the monthly or quarterly statements issued by the lender, along with the year-end 1098 form, which shows the total principal, interest and property tax paid for the year. All receipts for repairs or any improvements should be kept in the **Repairs** folder. Under **Taxes**, file the county tax assessor's statements (even if property taxes are paid out of the escrow account, you'll receive a statement of property tax liability). All documents relating to the property's fire, hazard and liability insurance should be kept in the **Insurance** folder. Under **Travel**, file receipts for any expenses relating to travel to and from the property: air fare, car rental, and mileage log. Receipts for express mail (such as Fedex, UPS, etc.), postage, or telephone can be filed under **Miscellaneous Expenses**.

The above system is very, very easy; once you've created your file folders, your primary job is to make sure that the right documents get filed in the right folders. When tax time comes around, having your documents organized in this manner will make the task much easier.

If you want to retain most of the documents via electronic means only, be sure to set up separate folders on your computer.

As your portfolio grows, organizing all the papers, statements and receipts relating to your investments becomes increasingly important. Separate files for each property will prevent confusion later. Even if you hold on to a property for 20 or 30 years, eventually you'll want to refinance, sell or exchange it, and you'll need to have the correct papers on hand. Holding onto the essential documents, like the Settlement Statement and the deed, is always a good idea. The ongoing records for management etc., can be discarded after a few years (please check with your accountant).

Using Quicken as Your Accounting System

Setting up computer software to record your income and expenses takes a little more time but provides an accounting function that can handle all the math for you, and offers the benefit of creating clear, concise reports and records for your files. In addition, you can transfer data from your Quicken account to your tax forms.

Even if you decide to use Quicken or a similar program to handle your accounting tasks, you'll still need to keep a paper file, as outlined above, for your documents and receipts. QuickBooks is the software preferred by most accountants, and your accountant may ask you to use it. It is more involved, powerful, and professional than Quicken. However, if this is just for your own records, Quicken may suffice to handle a certain amount of rental homes. Many of the tips we give below for Quicken apply generally to QuickBooks as well.

Getting Started

First, you'll need to set up a Quicken account, the basic file in which you'll post income and expenses. It looks much like a check register and, in fact, will mirror your investment checking account. Upon setting up the account, you'll enter the date your investment checking account was opened, and the amount of your first deposit.

Next, choose **Classes** from the View menu, and click on **New** to enter the address of your investment property. You don't have to enter the entire address, just enough to distinguish it from other properties, i.e., "Elm St.," or "Palm Ave."

Using the classes function in Quicken allows you to use one account to track all your properties—yet separate them for individual reports.

After creating a class for each of your properties, you'll want to create a list of categories. Categories track income and expenses by type, just as your file folders keep different types of expenses separate from each other. Quicken offers a list of pre-set categories, but I recommend setting up a customized list that includes only the categories you'll need for your investment properties.

Choose **Categories and Transfers** from the View Menu, then click the **New** button that appears in the dialog box. For your first category, type in "Rent." Below the Category name field, you'll see a box labeled Type and two buttons: **Income** and **Expense**. For the "rent" category, click on **Income**. "Rent" is the money that's flowing into your account. You may also want to create a second income category, called "Other Income" for any miscellaneous income items such as late fees from tenants, reimbursements, etc.

All other categories are **Expense** categories: the checks you write against the account. For each category, repeat this process: choose

Categories and Transfers from the View Menu, click the **New** button that appears in the dialog box, type in the name of the category, and click on **Expense**.

Create a list of the following categories (bold) and sub-categories (indented):

- **Mortgage Payment**

  Principal and Interest

  Taxes

  PMI

- **Auto & Travel**
- **Commissions**
- **Insurance**
- **Legal and other professional fees**
- **Management Fees**
- **Repairs**
- **Supplies**
- **Taxes**
- **Utilities**
- **Other**

You can use the categories listed on Schedule E (Form 1040) of the tax return. See Chapter 12.

Entering Transactions

Just as you enter deposits and withdrawals to your checking account, you'll enter all transactions in your Quicken account. The difference is that, by assigning classes and categories to each entry, you'll be able to generate reports that can add up your income and expenses by class (individual property), and/or by category, such as the total amount of principal, and interest paid to date.

As you work with Quicken, you may want to create more sub-categories to track your expenses, such as adding "Plumbing" or "Painting" under

"Repairs." You can get as detailed as you like. The main thing, though, is to create categories that reflect the types of tax deductions you can take on your investment properties (I'll address that in more detail in the next chapter).

Creating Reports

The time you spend entering data into your Quicken account will seem worthwhile once you see the result of your efforts printed out in a report. A report is simply a list of all transactions in either a class or a category. The report will add up all income and deduct expenses, giving you an instant bottom-line look at your investment.

Profit and Loss Statements

At the end of each year, you'll want to create a profit and loss statement. You can create a profit and loss statement for each property or combine them for an overview of all your investments. If you've been diligent about filing all your documents and receipts in the correct folders, you'll have the necessary numbers at your fingertips.

Below is an example of a P&L statement for a $170,000 property ($136,000 mortgage at 5%) that rents for $1,400 a month.

PROFIT & LOSS	
Income: (rent)	**$16,800.00**
Expenses:	
P&I:	**($8,760.00)**
Real Estate Taxes:	**($1,920.00)**
Insurance:	**($768.00)**
Property Management:	**(1,344.00)**
Repairs:	**($500.00)**
Miscellaneous:	**($1,000.00)**
Total Expenses:	**($14,292.00)**
Profit:	**$2,508.00**

Depreciation: Another Profit Booster

Let's assume that this $170,000 property has an improvement value of $136,000. The depreciation deduction would be approximately $4,945 per year. When you add the depreciation deduction to the profit and loss statement, you can claim a loss of $2,437, instead of an income of $2,508 for the year. If you're in the 32% tax bracket, this represents a tax savings of $1,582. If you have an annual adjusted gross income of less than $100,000 per year, you can deduct losses of up to $25,000 each year. If your adjusted gross income is more than $100,000 per year, the amount you can deduct for losses is reduced according to income. However, even those with high incomes can gain tax benefits by carrying forward their losses into another year. Of course, depreciation is recaptured upon sale. See Chapter 12 for details.

Updating Your Net Worth

Once you've completed your year-end profit and loss statement, you'll probably want to update your net worth worksheet.

How do your investments affect your net worth? One, by increasing the amount of cash on hand, in the form of profits from rentals and/or reduced taxes; and two, by appreciation and loan principal reduction, which create equity. These last two are elements that aren't typically noted on a profit and loss statement, and yet have great importance in terms of your net worth. Appreciation (if any) is the amount your property has increased in value. Equity is the difference between your loan balance and the property's market value.

Going back to the above example, let's assume you purchased the house in January and it's been rented for the entire year. You have already seen how you've made a profit of $2,508 in income, and $1,582 in tax savings). The principal on the $136,000 loan, however, has been paid down to $133,994. Let's assume the property has appreciated five percent, bringing its value up to $178,500. Your equity in the property is now $44,506—a $10,506 increase in one year.

Your $40,000 investment has increased your net worth by $10,506 in one year. That's over a 26% return on your money. And keep in mind that the first year is usually the least profitable (this, of course, ignores selling expenses if you were to sell, and only refers to the equity increase). As your property increases in value and rental prices rise (as, on average, they will with time), and the principal on the mortgage decreases at an ever-accelerating rate, your investment will reap far greater returns than this. Of course, this example looked only at the equity as expressed by the difference between the value of the home and the loan balance. If you were to sell, there would be significant sales expenses (commissions, closing costs etc.) that would decrease the NET equity. As the years go by, the selling expenses become even more negligible relative to the equity. Remember these are long term investments.

REPLAY

- ▶ Open a separate checking account for rental income and mortgage payments.
- ▶ Create a legal-size filing system.
- ▶ Keep all income and expenses separated by property.
- ▶ Use the Classes feature if you use Quicken (or QuickBooks) to keep information on each property separate while using one account.
- ▶ You can create a year-end profit and loss statement for each property, and/or combine for total profit and loss.
- ▶ Add depreciation deduction to profit and loss figures for a look at your after-tax profits.
- ▶ Include equity, attained by appreciation and loan principal reduction, in your updated net worth worksheet.

CHAPTER 12

SELLING, REFINANCING, AND TAX-RELATED ISSUES

There will probably be a time when you'll want to sell, refinance or trade one or more of your investment properties. Before taking this step, you'll need to know how this will affect your investment plan, income, and tax liability. Once you understand how rental income, deductions and depreciation affect your taxable income, you'll be able to make an informed decision about how to dispose of your property: whether to refinance, trade or sell.

Tax Preparation

The following is a general overview of current tax considerations. While this will give you an overall idea of how your real estate investments will affect your tax liability, I suggest using a tax preparer or a certified public accountant (CPA) to prepare your tax return. Tax laws are subject to change from year to year, and you'll need someone who's up on all the latest revisions. In addition, the fee you pay for tax preparation is deductible.

Tax Deductions for Rental Properties

Income and expenses for rental properties are reported on Schedule E, Supplemental Income and Loss, and attached to your income tax return.

Each Schedule E (see illustration) provides space for three properties. If you own more than three, simply use as many Schedule E forms as necessary. In Part 1, list the street address (including city and state) and type of property (i.e. "4233 Oak Street, Oklahoma City, Oklahoma, single-family residence, or SFH for brevity") On line 3, enter the total rents received for the tax year. The primary expense categories are shown on lines 5 through 17:

Advertising

Any costs associated with advertising your rental, such as newspaper advertisements, "For Rent" signs, and internet listings should be entered here. If you use a management company, the cost of advertising is included in the management fee and should be reported under "Management Fees" in line 11.

Auto and Travel

All travel to and from your property, lodging, and 50% of your meal expenses while traveling can be deducted. You can also include any travel in connection with your rental activities (i.e. travel to and from a meeting with your property manager). For auto expenses, you can either deduct actual expenses or the standard mileage rate. You must use actual expenses if you use more than one vehicle for your rental activities.

Cleaning and Maintenance

Payments made for housecleaning, landscaping, pool upkeep (recall I do not recommend buying houses with pools), pest control, or other maintenance services (chimney sweep, rain gutter cleaning) should be reported here.

SCHEDULE E
(Form 1040 or 1040-SR)

Department of the Treasury
Internal Revenue Service (99)

Supplemental Income and Loss

(From rental real estate, royalties, partnerships, S corporations, estates, trusts, REMICs, etc.)

▶ Attach to Form 1040, 1040-SR, 1040-NR, or 1041.

▶ Go to *www.irs.gov/ScheduleE* for instructions and the latest information.

OMB No. 1545-0074

2019

Attachment
Sequence No. **13**

Name(s) shown on return

Your social security number

Part I **Income or Loss From Rental Real Estate and Royalties** **Note:** If you are in the business of renting personal property, use **Schedule C** (see instructions). If you are an individual, report farm rental income or loss from **Form 4835** on page 2, line 40.

A Did you make any payments in 2019 that would require you to file Form(s) 1099? (see instructions) . . . . . ☐ Yes ☐ No

B If "Yes," did you or will you file required Forms 1099? . . . . ☐ Yes ☐ No

1a Physical address of each property (street, city, state, ZIP code)

A

B

C

1b Type of Property (from list below)	**2** For each rental real estate property listed above, report the number of fair rental and personal use days. Check the **QJV** box only if you meet the requirements to file as a qualified joint venture. See instructions.		**Fair Rental Days**	**Personal Use Days**	**QJV**
A		**A**			☐
B		**B**			☐
C		**C**			☐

Type of Property:

1 Single Family Residence 3 Vacation/Short-Term Rental 5 Land 7 Self-Rental

2 Multi-Family Residence 4 Commercial 6 Royalties 8 Other (describe)

Income:	**Properties:**		**A**	**B**	**C**
3 Rents received	**3**				
4 Royalties received	**4**				
Expenses:					
5 Advertising	**5**				
6 Auto and travel (see instructions)	**6**				
7 Cleaning and maintenance	**7**				
8 Commissions.	**8**				
9 Insurance	**9**				
10 Legal and other professional fees	**10**				
11 Management fees	**11**				
12 Mortgage interest paid to banks, etc. (see instructions)	**12**				
13 Other interest.	**13**				
14 Repairs.	**14**				
15 Supplies	**15**				
16 Taxes	**16**				
17 Utilities.	**17**				
18 Depreciation expense or depletion	**18**				
19 Other (list) ▶ _____	**19**				
20 Total expenses. Add lines 5 through 19	**20**				
21 Subtract line 20 from line 3 (rents) and/or 4 (royalties). If result is a (loss), see instructions to find out if you must file **Form 6198**	**21**				
22 Deductible rental real estate loss after limitation, if any, on **Form 8582** (see instructions)	**22**	( )(	)(	)	

23a Total of all amounts reported on line 3 for all rental properties	**23a**			
b Total of all amounts reported on line 4 for all royalty properties	**23b**			
c Total of all amounts reported on line 12 for all properties	**23c**			
d Total of all amounts reported on line 18 for all properties	**23d**			
e Total of all amounts reported on line 20 for all properties	**23e**			
24 **Income.** Add positive amounts shown on line 21. **Do not** include any losses	**24**		
25 **Losses.** Add royalty losses from line 21 and rental real estate losses from line 22. Enter total losses here .	**25**	(	)
26 **Total rental real estate and royalty income or (loss).** Combine lines 24 and 25. Enter the result here. If Parts II, III, IV, and line 40 on page 2 do not apply to you, also enter this amount on Schedule 1 (Form 1040 or 1040-SR), line 5, or Form 1040-NR, line 18. Otherwise, include this amount in the total on line 41 on page 2	**26**		

For Paperwork Reduction Act Notice, see the separate instructions. Cat. No. 11344L Schedule E (Form 1040 or 1040-SR) 2019

Commissions

If you sell your property, agent's commissions are entered here, along with lender commissions for refinancing.

Insurance

Include all premiums for fire, casualty and liability insurance.

Legal and Other Professional Fees

Tax advice, tax preparation and costs incurred for tenant eviction, or other legal consultations regarding your properties, would be entered here.

Management Fees

Include all property management fees including those for lease negotiation.

Mortgage Interest

If you paid interest to a bank or other financial institution, you should receive a 1098 Form showing the total interest paid for that year.

Other Interest

If you received a loan from a friend or relative that was used to purchase the property, enter the total annual interest payment under "other interest." Be sure you have documentation—a contract and cancelled checks—to substantiate your deduction.

Repairs

According to the IRS, a repair is something that keeps your property in good working condition but does not add significantly to its value or prolong its life. Conversely, a capital improvement increases the value of your property and extends its life.

If you use a property management company, they should provide you with an itemized list of all repairs made to your property. Enter the total amount spent for repairs.

Supplies

If you purchase cleaning supplies, tools, etc. for the maintenance of your property, you can deduct their actual cost.

Taxes

If property taxes are paid from your escrow account, the amount paid will be itemized on the 1098 Form you receive from the mortgage company. Otherwise, check the county tax assessor's statement for the total amount of taxes paid.

Utilities

You can deduct the cost of telephone calls related to your rental activities.

Depreciation

Depreciation is a deduction the government allows you to take to recover the cost of investment property that has a life beyond the tax year. For residential property, depreciation is deducted over a 27.5-year period. Land is not depreciable. Depreciation for less than a year is proportional to the amount of time out of the year you owned the property. On the next page is a table showing the depreciation amount for the first year, based on which month of the year you acquired the property. It starts from the middle of each month:

FIRST YEAR DEPRECIATION PERCENTAGES			
JAN	FEB	MAR	APR
3.485	3.182	2.879	2.576
MAY	JUN	JUL	AUG
2.273	1.970	1.667	1.364
SEP	OCT	NOV	DEC
1.061	0.758	0.455	0.152

Repairs and Capital Improvements

As noted above, repairs are fully deductible expenses defined, generally, as an expense to keep the property operational. Capital improvements increase the improvement value of the property and lengthen its useful life. For example, if you patch a hole in a wall, that's a *repair*; if you add a room with new walls, that's a *capital improvement*. Capital improvements can be depreciated over a long period. These lengths change from time to time. This is an issue on which it's best to follow the advice of your tax preparer.

Profit and Loss

If your rental income is greater than your expenses and depreciation deduction, you'll show a profit that will be added to your taxable income and entered on the 1040 Form. If you have a loss, you'll be able to subtract it from your taxable income, with certain limitations.

Passive Activity Loss Rules

Rental real estate is considered a passive investment, and as such is subject to passive loss limitations. In general, this means passive losses are deductible only against passive income, such as the income you earn from real estate. The tax law allows for certain exceptions, however. You can claim passive losses of up to $25,000 per year against your active income (wages, salary, etc.) if you meet the requirements for active participation. Happily, you can meet these requirements without regular or continuous involvement in your real estate activities—if you are responsible for significant decisions affecting your properties.

As defined by the IRS (and please always check with your accountant, as these definitions can be modified over time), you can meet the active participation requirements even when a property management company is handling your property, since you'll be making management decisions such as approving new tenants, deciding on rental terms, and authorizing capital or repair expenditures.

In addition to active participation, you must meet a few other requirements:

- **Rental real estate activities are your only passive activities.**

- **You do not have any prior year un-allowed losses from passive activities.**

- **You have no current or prior year un-allowed credits from passive activities.**

- **Your modified adjusted gross income is $100,000 or less ($50,000 or less if married filing separately).**

If your modified adjusted gross income is $100,000 or less, you can deduct up to $25,000 in losses each year. If your modified adjusted gross income is more than $100,000, the amount of passive loss you can deduct is reduced incrementally according to income. Between $100,000 and $150,000 (for married couples), the passive loss exception is reduced 50 cents for every dollar your adjusted gross income exceeds $100,000 (see table).

Suspended Losses

If your adjusted gross income is more than $150,000, don't fret. Even if you're currently unable to claim passive losses against your active income, you can "carry forward" the losses from year to year.

Under current tax law, you can carry forward real estate investment losses. Please check with your accountant to see if and when these might expire in the future. The losses accrue each year, building up a kind of "savings account" of losses. When you sell or otherwise dispose of a property, these losses can be used to offset any gain. MAGI stands for Modified Gross Adjusted Income.

PASSIVE ACTIVITY LOSS ALLOWANCE	
Income (MAGI)	Loss Allowance
$100,000	$25,000
$105,000	$22,500
$110,000	$20,000
$115,000	$17,500
$120,000	$15,000
$125,000	$12,500
$130,000	$10,000
$135,000	$7,500
$140,000	$5,000
$145,000	$2,500
$150,000	$0

Exception for Real Estate Professionals

If you work in a real estate trade or business at least 750 hours per year (about 14 hours per week), and more than one-half of the total personal services you perform in these trades or businesses are performed in real property trades or businesses in which you materially participate, you may be exempt from passive loss rules and may deduct passive losses against your taxable income without limitations.

Essentially, this is a special tax shelter for those in the real estate business, including real estate agents, loan brokers, property managers, and owners of rental properties. You don't need an agent's or broker's license, but you must meet the minimum annual hourly requirement. Recall that more than one-half of the services you perform each year must fall within the definition of the real estate trade: buying and selling property, making loans, investing in properties, property management or construction.

The Tax Law of 2018

At the beginning of 2018 a new tax law was passed. Most of the existing tax structures and benefits discussed for real estate investors within this chapter did not change. However, the law did include an addition favorable to real estate investors called "The Pass-Through Deduction," which can limit taxable income to 80% of what it was before the new tax law on certain real estate investments held in common forms.

Under the 2018 tax plan, taxpayers who itemize will be able to deduct their state individual income tax, as well as sales and property taxes, up to a limit of $10,000 in total starting in 2018.

For 2018-2025, the current tax plan generally allows you to deduct interest on up to $750,000 of mortgage debt incurred to buy or improve a first or second residence (so-called home acquisition debt), down from $1,000,000 previously.

This has created a bit of a panic in metropolitan areas with high home prices, like San Francisco, Los Angeles and New York. However, for the Sun Belt states' metropolitan areas in which we invest, these limits are not likely to have any effect, and the new deductions only enhance the attractiveness of being a real estate investor. I have already met people who have decided they will not own their own home in San Francisco or New York City, but rent their residence in those cities, where rents are actually low relative to the home prices and invest in rental homes in the affordable markets in the Sun Belt states instead.

Realizing Profits from Your Investments

When most people hear the word "profit" in conjunction with real estate investing, they assume it means selling property. But if you've followed the strategy in this book and have purchased relatively new, high quality properties in good markets and good locations, selling might be the least attractive method to realize gains from your investment.

Why? When you sell, four things happen:

- **You pay taxes.**

- **You pay agents' commissions.**

- **You lose an appreciating asset.**

- **You may be paying off a 30-year fixed rate loan rather than let inflation continue to erode it.**

For all these reasons, selling incurs costs that can't be recovered. However, there are other ways to take cash out of your property or to leverage it for another investment without all these costs.

Refinancing

If you need cash for some reason—like college tuition or a major expense—refinancing or taking out an equity loan on your property offers a low-cost way to raise money. Interest on a new first mortgage, second mortgage or equity loan is tax-deductible for an investment property, and the extra mortgage interest paid will offset your rental income. This will reduce the property's bottom line, and add less passive income to your earned income, which will reduce your taxes.

Here's an example of a typical property over 15 years, and the monetary consequences of both selling and refinancing:

YEAR 2020	
Original price:	**$170,000**
Loan amount:	$136,000
Monthly payments:	
Principal and Interest:	$730
Taxes:	$161
Insurance:	$65
Property Management:	$120
Total:	$1,076
Monthly Rent:	**$1,400**

As you can see, this property started out with a positive monthly cash flow of $324 a month, which adds up to an annual positive cash flow of $3,888 before repairs and vacancy. If we take repairs (minimal on new homes) and vacancy to total $150/month, the yearly net profit becomes $2,088. With the annual depreciation deduction of approximately $3,600, however, you can declare an annual loss of $1,512. If you're in the 32% tax bracket, that's an in-your-pocket profit of $1,152 the first year—which raises the overall positive cash flow.

After 15 years, the numbers on the property undergo a profound change:

YEAR 2035	
Original price:	**$170,000**
Current value:	$306,160 (rising 4% annually)
Original Loan amount:	$136,000 @ 5%
Loan balance:	$92,323
Monthly payments:	
Principal and Interest:	$730
Taxes, rising 4% annually:	$290
Insurance, rising 4% annually:	$117
Property Management:	$174
Total:	$1,311
Monthly Rent:	**$2,181** (rising 3% annually)
Equity:	**$213,837**

After 15 years, the property has built up over $200,000 in equity and is generating profits of $870 per month, or $10,441 per year. Say you want to cash out now. How much money will you actually receive?

Let's assume the house sells for its current market price of $306,000. You will pay a commission of 6% ($18,360) and closing costs of about $3,000. After paying off the balance of the original loan, you're left with capital gains of approximately $192,000.

The capital gains rate (as of 2020), is 15% for most taxpayers (except the highest tax bracket payers for which it is 20%, and 0% for the bottom two tax brackets). This is a favorable rate compared to capital gains tax in past years; however, not all states are compliant with capital gains tax rates. For example, California does not use capital gains tax rates: all capital gains are taxed as income, according to your tax bracket. As we all know, taxes are the first thing to come straight off the top of your profit: you must assume 15% is the very least you'll pay. So, your $192,000 is reduced $28,800 by capital gains taxes at 15%. In addition, you must pay taxes on depreciation recapture: the depreciation you have deducted over the past 15 years is added up and taxed at your marginal income tax bracket, but not to exceed 25%. (Used here because it will be the amount for most investors.) For the above example, the depreciation deductions taken over 15 years add up to $73,636 (assuming an improvement value of $135,000). A 25% tax on this amount is $18,409.

So, what do you have left over after the sale is final? $144,791.

Certainly, $144,791 in the hand is better than a kick in the head, but, at a minimum you'll spend close to $50,000 to get it. Last but not least: you no longer have an appreciating asset, one that could, in the next 10 to 15 years, rise in value another $200,000 or more. Of course, you also just paid off a miraculous 30-year fixed rate loan, which never keeps up with inflation, just as it is entering the part of its life when principal payments begin to become very meaningful.

In contrast, here's what happens when you refinance:

YEAR 2035	
Original price:	**$170,000**
Current value:	$306,160 (rising 4% annually)
Original Loan amount:	$136,000 @ 5%
Loan balance:	$92,323
New Loan:	$214,000
Monthly payments:	
New Loan Principal and Interest:	$1,148.79
Taxes, rising 4% annually:	$289.95
Insurance, rising 4% annually:	$117
Property Management:	$174
Total:	**$1,730**
Monthly Rent:	**$2,181** (rising 3% annually)
Monthly Cash Flow:	**$451**
Cash Out:	**$121,000**
Equity:	**$92,160**

Even *with the new mortgage* payment, the property has a positive monthly cash flow of $451 before the unknown expenses of repairs, vacancy, etc.–that is $5,412 each year. And since your depreciation deduction is still $3,600, you'll be able to reduce your taxable income to $1,812.

For a cost of 3% to 5% of the loan amount (in the above example, about $3,000 to $5,000), you've raised $121,000 on which you don't have to pay taxes. You also have $92,000 equity remaining in the property, and an appreciating asset that will continue to generate profits, tax savings, and increase your net worth. Of course, the new

30-year fixed rate loan will continue the magic of being eroded by inflation for many more years into your future.

Trading to Defer Taxes: The 1031 Exchange

In a tax-deferred exchange, real property can be traded without tax liability (which gets deferred). In other words, instead of selling your property and paying taxes, you can use all the equity in your property to trade for another property (or properties), without taking the big tax bite (until the possible later sale of the replacement properties). You can think of it as an equity preservation program that works through reinvestment.

Typically, the person you sell property to is not the one you're buying from, which means most exchanges are three-party affairs: you, the person who buys your property, and the person(s) you buy property (or properties) from. Once your property is sold, you have 45 days to identify the replacement property (or properties), and 180 days (starting on the same date as the 45 days) to complete the acquisition of the new property (or properties).

There are a few parameters that must be adhered to:

- **Traded properties must be of "like kind."** This rule is interpreted broadly, but it generally means both properties must be held for investment or use in one's trade or business.

- **Property acquired must be of equal or greater value to the net sale price of property sold.** (The "net sale price" is the sale price minus closing costs and broker's fee.)

- **Properties must be in the U.S.**

- **Typically, the entire net sale proceeds go toward the acquisition of the replacement property.** In cases where the exchanger receives cash, personal property or other assets in the exchange, it is taxable.

- **An intermediary is used to facilitate the exchange and hold funds during the period between sale and acquisition** The exchanger is not allowed possession of the funds in the interim.

The point of the 1031 exchange is to avoid depletion of the equity you've already built up, and to avoid capital gains tax. The 1031 exchange allows you to reinvest that equity without presently paying taxes, if you do it within a specific time frame, and according to specific rules. The rules for tax-deferred exchanges can be complex and exacting, so it's best to consult a specialist before moving ahead. That said, it's an excellent way to rollover your equity into another investment (for example, to trade in an older property for a newer one, or several new ones, that will have greater depreciation, a longer functional life, fewer repairs, and higher rental rates). You can use equity from one property to reinvest in several properties or consolidate several less expensive properties into a more expensive one.

Selling Your Property

I've saved selling for last because, in my view, there are only a few good reasons to sell an investment property. The benefits of holding onto the property—or refinancing or exchanging it—are often greater in the long run. However, there are some circumstances under which you may find it prudent to sell your property.

It's a dog: It's a fact of life that some properties are bad. If you're having a hard time keeping it rented, it needs lots of repairs, and you're losing money, get rid of it.

You need cash: If, for some reason, you need an instant influx of all the money you can get your hands on, you may have no choice but to sell.

There is a clear boom (bubble): if there is a clear period of a boom, which creates a distinct sellers' market in the metropolitan area in which you own, it may be a good idea to sell. Of course, it still is possible to sell in a booming market and do a 1031 exchange into several rental homes in a market that is not booming at the time. A booming, "bubble" market may have enticing elements for the seller such as: multiple offers, prices exceeding the asking price, or quick sales. A good example is the period of 2005-2006, which created strong bubbles in various markets such as Las Vegas, Phoenix, large metropolitan areas in California,

Florida, Georgia, and others. At the same time, Texas and Oklahoma did not boom. I had many investors sell one home in Phoenix and exchange it for three or four homes in Dallas or Oklahoma City at that time.

Suspended losses: If you have been unable to claim passive losses because of a high taxable income, and these losses will greatly reduce the amount of capital gains realized from the sale, selling may be more to your advantage than refinancing or exchanging.

Stepped-Up Cost Basis

When an asset is inherited upon the death of its original owner, it is often worth more than when it was originally purchased. In order to prevent a potentially large capital gains tax bill upon the sale of inherited property, the cost basis of the asset in question is changed to its value at the time of its owner's death, a concept known as a step-up in basis.

One important distinction is that this concept only applies to property transferred after death. If any property was gifted or transferred before the original owner dies, the original cost basis would transfer to the inheritor.

As a simplified example, let's say that your uncle bought shares of a certain stock in the 1990s, and that he originally paid $50 per share. You inherit the stock in 2020, and it's now trading for $300 per share. For capital gains tax purposes, the IRS would calculate any future gains as if you had paid $300 per share for the stock, not the $50 that was *actually* paid for it.

If the stock had been sold the day before your uncle died, there would be a $250 taxable capital gain per share (assuming that it was owned in a non-retirement account). If it was sold just the day after you inherited it, there would be no taxable gain whatsoever. If you hold the stock for a while, any capital gains tax would only be assessed on any difference between the eventual sale price and $300.

It's important to note that step-up in basis can allow heirs to avoid capital gains taxes. However, it does *not* allow heirs to avoid estate taxes that apply to large inheritances.

In 2020, the estate tax is levied on property in excess of $11.58 million per individual ($23.16 million per married couple). In other words, if you and your spouse leave a $26 million estate to your heirs, $2.84 million of this amount will still be taxable, even though your heirs' *cost basis* in assets they inherited will be stepped up for capital gains tax purposes.

There may be ways to avoid estate taxes with appropriate planning, but step-up in basis doesn't exclude the value of inherited property from a taxable estate all by itself.

For real estate, there are two benefits: First, just like with any other asset, you don't have to pay capital gains on any appreciation that occurred before you inherited the property. Selling an investment property after a long holding period can result in a *big* capital gains tax bill, so this can be a very valuable benefit.

The other side is that a step-up in basis can give you a bigger depreciation tax benefit. The cost basis of residential real estate can be depreciated over a period of 27.5 years (structure only, not the land). Obviously, a higher number divided by 27.5 years is a greater annual depreciation deduction than a smaller number would produce.

For example, let's say that you inherit a property that your parents purchased 20 years ago for $100,000. It is now worth about $400,000. Assuming $300,000 is the depreciable value (total value minus land cost), not only does a $400,000 cost basis translate to a $10,909 annual depreciation deduction on the $300,000 value of the structure, but you can take this deduction every year throughout the full 27.5-year depreciation period even though the previous owner likely claimed depreciation deductions for the 20 years they owned it. Secondly, you won't have to pay a penny of capital gains tax on the $300,000 increase in value that occurred while your parents owned it.

Thus, in the case of real estate, the provision is very beneficial.

This is one of the reasons there are so many investors who contact me in their 60s, 70s, and even 80s, wanting to begin buying rental homes. Even the 80+ year-olds know that if and when they pass away, the properties will transfer to their heirs on a stepped-up basis, to continue improving their heirs' financial futures without being taxed (and adding new depreciation the heirs can deduct).

Please verify everything with your tax person, and keep abreast of any developments. There has been talk in the past of possibly modifying or eliminating the step-up in basis upon death. It has endured, but make sure by asking.

REPLAY

- ► Gain a thorough understanding of rental property tax law to make the most of deductions and depreciation.
- ► Use a tax preparer or CPA who has a knowledge of real estate tax law to prepare your tax return.
- ► If your adjusted gross income is under $100,000, you can deduct up to $25,000 a year in passive losses against active income.
- ► Suspended losses can be "rolled-over" and subtracted from capital gains realized from sale of property later.
- ► Real estate professionals can possibly claim unlimited losses, subject to certain provisions.
- ► Selling your property incurs unrecoverable costs.
- ► Refinancing offers tax-free cash.
- ► Consider a 1031 exchange before selling.
- ► If there is a clear boom/bubble, consider selling.
- ► The step-up in basis applies to properties passed to heirs upon an owner's death. The basis gets stepped-up to the value at the time of death.

GLOSSARY

Airbnb
An online marketplace which lets people rent out their properties or spare rooms to guests

Adjustable Rate Loan (ARM)
A loan with a variable interest rate that rises or falls according to the index to which it is tied.

Adjusted Gross Income
Your taxable income after deductions.

Annual Percentage Rate (APR)
This reflects the true annual cost of a loan. The APR is determined by adding the interest rate to the loan fees and is expressed as a percentage.

Appraisal
An estimate of property value produced by an independent appraiser.

Appreciation
The increase of property value.

Capital Gains
The taxable profits derived from the sale or exchange of a capital asset, such as real property.

Cash Flow
The difference between expenses and income. For example, if a property has an income of $10,000 and expenses of $4,000, it has a $6,000 positive cash flow. If expenses are $12,000, it has a $2,000 negative cash flow.

Closing
Also known as Settlement. Closing is the act of finalizing all arrangements between the buyer and seller. Money is disbursed, the deed is prepared in the new owner's name, and the property is conveyed in accordance with the contract signed by both parties.

Closing Costs
The fees associated with the closing of escrow, or of a loan.

Coronavirus
Coronaviruses are a type of virus. There are many different kinds, and some cause disease. A newly identified coronavirus, SARS-CoV-2, has caused a worldwide pandemic of respiratory illness, called COVID-19.

COVID-19
COVID-19 an infectious disease caused by a coronavirus discovered in 2019/2020.

Depreciation
Loss against the property (for tax purposes only), prorated over 27.5 years for residential property.

Equity
The cash value of a property, less any outstanding mortgages and liens.

Escrow
A trust account wherein deposit money is held by a neutral third party (usually an escrow officer or title company) prior to finalization of the sale. When escrow is "closed," it means the transaction has been completed: the seller is paid, and the buyer takes title to the property.

Fixed-Rate Loan
A loan with an interest rate that does not change over the life of the loan.

Flip
To sell a property soon after buying it (ideally for a quick profit.)

Foreclosure
When a property owner defaults on the mortgage and the lender takes possession of the property.

Hybrid Loan
A loan which combines an Adjustable Rate Loan (ARM) and Fixed-Rate Loan.

Improvement Value
The cost of the property less the cost of the land. When you take a depreciation deduction, you may only take depreciation against the cost of the structure, not the land. The structure is also known as the "improvements."

Interest
What lenders charge for the use of their money. Interest is expressed as a percentage, or interest rate, which is a factor of the APR.

Leverage
To borrow and use other people's money, generally a bank's or lending institution's.

Lien
A claim against property, which can include mortgages, trusts, and unpaid property taxes. The primary purpose of a title search is to be certain all liens are known at the day of settlement.

Market
An area, usually defined by city, in which to invest.

Median Price
Median means "in the middle." So, with regard to List Price, this means exactly half of homes listed are above this price and exactly half are below. For example, let's say there are 5 homes for sale in a market at prices of $175,000, $200,000, $250,000, $350,000, and $600,000. The median price would be the one in the middle, or $250,000.

Net Worth
The wealth you've accumulated to date (i.e. what's left after subtracting your liabilities from your assets).

No Money Down
Can also be thought of as 100% financing. If you borrow money for the down payment, then you have purchased a property with 100% financing, or no money down.

Pandemic
A disease prevalent over a whole country or the world.

Pass-Through Deduction
The Tax Cuts and Jobs Act (HR 1, "TCJA") established a new tax deduction for owners of pass-through businesses. Pass-through owners who qualify can deduct up to 20% of their net business income from their income taxes, reducing their effective income tax rate by 20%. This deduction began in 2018 and is scheduled to last through 2025—that is, it will end on January 1, 2026 unless extended by Congress.

Points
An up-front fee paid to the lender at closing. One point equals 1% of the loan amount (i.e. one point of a $100,000 loan would be $1000).

Principal
The loan amount, which is paid off in part each month along with the interest payment.

Private Mortgage Insurance (PMI)
When you make a down payment of less than 20%, lenders require you carry private mortgage insurance, or PMI. PMI protects lenders from financial loss if the homeowner goes into Foreclosure.

Profit & Loss Statement
An accounting of your investment's income and expenses, which will show either profit or loss.

Property Manager
For a fee (generally between 8% and 10% of the gross rent collected) a property manager can handle all aspects of renting and maintaining your investment property, from leasing to repairs.

Refinance
To secure new financing for a property, whether by securing a new first mortgage, an equity loan, or a second mortgage.

Repair
Repairs are fully deductible expenses for items and services that keep the property operational. These are sometimes confused with Capital Improvements, which are different (see definition).

Retirement Account
A long-term savings and investment account. Popular retirement accounts include IRAs, 401(k)s and Keogh plans.

Return
The amount of profit realized from an investment. For example, if you make $4,000 on a $10,000 investment, that's a 40% return.

Settlement
See Closing.

Single-Family Home
A single-family home is a single unit, detached dwelling with a yard.

Stepped-Up Cost Basis
The cost basis of property transferred at death receives a "step-up" in basis to its fair market value. This eliminates an heir's capital gains tax liability on appreciation in the property's value that occurred during the decedent's lifetime.

FINAL WORDS

I have discussed in this book why buying single-family rental homes is a superior investment, especially for the busy person (which most of us are).

I have talked about the benefits of buying single-family homes using the unique 30-year fixed rate financing that is available ONLY in the United States, to the best of my knowledge. (Foreigners are amazed that we can get loans where nothing keeps up with inflation for as long as 30 years, meaning inflation keeps eroding the real value of our debt while the tenant is gradually paying it off for us). The 30-year fixed-rate mortgage is only available on 1-4 residential units, making single-family home rental investments even more attractive.

I covered how owning a portfolio of single-family rental homes can change everyone's financial future. It can facilitate putting your kids or grandkids through college. It can enable you to retire sooner and well. Overall, it can create a financial safety net for your future and the future of your family.

I discussed the benefits of buying these single-family homes in big cities in the Sun Belt states that are not booming, and where the median price is affordable, and the rent to value ratio is favorable to the investor.

Also covered was the infrastructure/ecosystem that our company, ICG, has set up in many large metropolitan areas in the Sun Belt. Our infrastructure includes local property managers and knowledgeable local brokers, as well as their own network of repair people, title companies, lenders, etc. Even though you buy the house in your own name, the service providers know we are watching. For example, in a market where all our investors have bought over 1,000 homes in the past 15 years, the managers know that if you are unhappy and we at ICG hear about it, they risk losing 1,000 homes, not just the one you bought. Thus we "lend you our clout" which strengthens your hand as an owner living in another state.

Working with our ecosystem, you can begin building a better financial future for yourself, regardless of how busy you might be. You can get started right now.

NEXT STEPS

After you have read this book, please take the first step to start buying your single-family home rental. Simply send us an email with your phone number at info@icgre.com. Our staff will call you to set up a phone meeting, quite possibly directly with me.

If you wish to call instead, please call us at (800) 324-3983. If you're calling from outside the U.S., call us in the San Francisco Bay Area at (415) 927-7504.

If you find yourself extra motivated to take the next step and want to see the variety of single-family home rentals currently available to our investors, please visit icgre.com. There you can join our "Quick Send List" and receive new property sheets as soon as we get them from our market teams nationwide. You will also get information about events and new markets. While at our site, you can see the schedule of our quarterly ICG 1-Day Expos.

Hopefully, you will plan to join us in person soon. People fly in from around the country to attend our Expos, usually held next to the San Francisco Airport. There you'll meet the teams from various markets who present key demographic and economic information about their markets to all in attendance. They'll show you the homes they have available at that moment. You'll learn about important issues such as buying single-family homes within a self-directed IRA, asset preservation & protection, tax issues for investors, the mechanics of 1031 tax-deferred exchanges, overall financial planning, and many other subjects of value. We bring experts in these fields to teach us at these events. You'll meet mortgage brokers licensed to fund investor loans in all fifty states. You will listen to and can participate in extensive and deep Q&A sessions, plus hear a lot of information from yours truly. You'll meet investors who have been working with the ICG infrastructure for years. It's all there. All you need to do is decide to join us for the day. Of course, during the pandemic, our amazing Expos have been online events, via Zoom, and are recorded and available on our website. In addition, I generate a newsletter every two months, and they are also available on our website (icgre.com under "resources"), for your convenience.

QUARTERLY EXPOS

There is an admission fee to attend. However, simply by mentioning this book when you email or call us, you can attend for **FREE**. Just email us at **info@icgre.com** and provide your name and tell us which Expo you want to attend. If you wish to bring a guest, please provide your guest's name as well, and they can also attend for free. While the Expos are online, the events are free for all. All you need to do to register yourself and your guests is simply go to **icgre.com/events** and register for free.

I can't wait to hear from you and I look forward to meeting you soon!

—Adiel Gorel

ABOUT THE AUTHOR

Adiel Gorel has more than three decades of successful real estate investing experience. As the CEO of ICG (International Capital Group) Real Estate, a world-renowned real estate investment firm founded in the San Francisco Bay Area in 1987, Gorel has helped investors utilize one of the most powerful investment tools—real estate. He teaches people how to have fun with a process most find complex and speaks about the importance of securing a strong financial future for retirement, business investing, and college education.

Through ICG, he has assisted thousands of investors, from novice to expert, in purchasing over 10,000 properties to date. He is also the author of *Invest Then Rest: How to Buy Single-Family Rental Properties*, which includes numerous investor reports describing their real-life investing experiences.

For over 30 years, ICG has hosted a 1-Day Expo each quarter, bringing expert speakers, market teams from all over the country, and hundreds of investors to the San Francisco Bay Area. ICG has an infrastructure of teams nationwide, supporting their investors.

Gorel has been featured on NBC, ABC, in *Fortune Magazine*, the *San Francisco Examiner*, and numerous radio shows showcasing his no-nonsense, insightful approach to real estate investing. He speaks worldwide and throughout the U.S., sharing his knowledge on a variety of topics including securing a powerful financial future, investing in single-family homes, the 30-year fixed-rate mortgage, and related subjects.

Adiel has created a Public Television special called "Remote Control Retirement Riches," as well as another Public Television show called "Life 201." He is also the author, with expert partners, of the book *Life 201*. Both TV shows have aired hundreds of times in large parts of the United States.

ICG has established an infrastructure to support investors in many metropolitan areas in the U.S. Gorel owns many properties himself.

To this day, Gorel supports individual investors via planning, assistance in remote home buying, and property management issues resolution.

He holds a master's degree from Stanford University. His professional experience includes being a Hewlett-Packard research engineer, as well as management and director positions at Excel Telecommunications and several biotechnology firms. He lives in the San Francisco Bay Area.

INDEX

Made in the USA
Las Vegas, NV
12 March 2023

68993305R00118